Evangelism
after
Pluralism

Evangelism after Pluralism

THE ETHICS OF CHRISTIAN WITNESS

BRYAN STONE

B
Baker Academic
a division of Baker Publishing Group
Grand Rapids, Michigan

Published by Baker Academic
a division of Baker Publishing Group
PO Box 6287, Grand Rapids, MI 49516-6287
www.bakeracademic.com

Printed in the United States of America

Library of Congress Cataloging-in-Publication Data
Names: Stone, Bryan P., 1959– author.
Title: Evangelism after pluralism : the ethics of Christian witness / Bryan Stone.
Description: Grand Rapids : Baker Publishing Group, 2018. | Includes bibliographical
    references and index.
Identifiers: LCCN 2017051466 | ISBN 9780801099793 (pbk. : alk. paper)
Subjects: LCSH: Missions. | Evangelistic work. | Cultural pluralism—Religious
    aspects—Christianity.
Classification: LCC BV2063 .S825 2018 | DDC 266—dc23
LC record available at https://lccn.loc.gov/2017051466

In keeping with biblical principles of creation stewardship, Baker Publishing Group advocates the responsible use of our natural resources. As a member of the Green Press Initiative, our company uses recycled paper when possible. The text paper of this book is composed in part of post-consumer waste.

18   19   20   21   22   23   24   7   6   5   4   3   2   1

Contents

Acknowledgments

The idea of pursuing something like an "ethics of evangelism" arose from a conversation I had with Rev. Grayson Lucky, formerly the pastor of Nichols Hills United Methodist Church in Oklahoma City. After reading my *Evangelism after Christendom*, Grayson made the observation that he saw it as resembling something like an "ethics of evangelism." That sounded exactly right to me. He and his congregation invited me to give their annual Pope Lecture Series in 2008, and I committed myself to furthering the project of developing an ethics of evangelism with more intentionality in that lecture series. While it has been almost a decade now, I am grateful to Grayson and the Nichols Hills church for their hospitality and for the opportunity afforded me to think further about the practice of evangelism in various contexts, especially in relation to pluralism.

I am indebted to my students and colleagues who have heard forms of these chapters in lectures or read sections in various venues and given valuable feedback. I especially wish to thank Emily Kleidon and Michelle Ashley for their valuable assistance in preparing the manuscript, and I am grateful to them both for their efficiency and attention to detail.

1

Competing for Space in the World

In his profound book *Christ on Trial*, Rowan Williams explores the various accounts of Christ's trial in each of the four Gospels. What surfaces in those accounts, especially in the Gospel of Mark, which highlights Jesus's silence before both the Sanhedrin and Pilate, is how Jesus stands outside the structures and languages of power by which he is being judged and how little leverage he has in that world. Says Williams,

> The world Mark depicts is not a reasonable one; it is full of demons and suffering and abused power. How, in such a world, *could* there be a language in which it could truly be said who Jesus is? Whatever is said will take on the colouring of the world's insanity; it will be another bid for the world's power, another identification with the unaccountable tyrannies that decide how things shall be. Jesus, described in the words of this world, would be a competitor for space in it, part of its untruth. (2000, 6)

To say with Williams that Jesus is not "a competitor for space" in the world is not to say that Jesus is distant or removed from the world, but rather that in his life the maps by which we order

1

our social relations are being redrawn. As Williams puts it, Jesus threatens "because he does not compete . . . and because it is that whole world of rivalry and defence which is in question" (69).

One of the great challenges of faithfully bearing Christian witness in our world is the way prevailing political, social, intellectual, and economic frameworks are granted the power to impose conditions on the Christian social imagination and thereby to constrict it so that we imagine our witness only within those frameworks and their accompanying stories, habits, practices, and social patterns. Evangelism becomes a practice competing for space in the world and, to use Williams's words, "part of its untruth" (6). The pacifist logic of evangelism as an offer of good news that empties itself of power and privilege is transformed into a logic of competition, exchange, and production that claws at the levers of power and lays claim to truth as a possession. As Williams says, quoting from Anita Mason's novel *The Illusionist*, "There is a kind of truth which, when it is said, becomes untrue" (Mason 1984, 6).[1]

If Williams is right, this is a sobering truth for would-be evangelists. Bearing faithful witness to Christ may mean that, more often than not, we are left with the challenge of how to communicate Christ's silence. This situation makes the task of contextualization in evangelism so demanding and risky, however unavoidable that task remains. In attempting to secure a space for the good news, we are tempted to compete for that space by accepting the terms of a false competition. We want the good news to be received positively in any given context, and we want it to make a difference in people's lives and in the world. We want what we have to say to be meaningful but also irresistible (cf. Yoder 1992). So we attempt to mitigate the gospel's strangeness, smoothing off its rough edges, securing its validity on the world's terms, and

1. George Lindbeck makes a similar point when he observes that "the crusader's battle cry 'Christus est Dominus,' [Christ is Lord] is false when used to authorize cleaving the skull of the infidel (even though the same words in other contexts may be a true utterance)" (1984, 64).

laying claim to structures of truth, power, and legitimacy that will shore up its credibility or attractiveness. We defend it using the rationalities and moralities that present themselves to us in our culture; ally it to structures of sovereignty, patriarchy, and privilege; or demonstrate its usefulness in achieving the social and economic goals of those to whom we would commend it. The good news is a gift. But when the good news is imposed imperially, defended with intellectually airtight arguments, or subjected to the logic of marketplace exchanges, the gift is no longer a gift. The ethics of evangelism, an ethics that is fundamentally self-emptying, gratuitous, and pacifist, becomes instead an ethics of conquering, defending, securing, and grasping.

Because Christians hope to secure a space in the world for the good news, there may be no Christian practice more susceptible to distortion than evangelism. Church growth, power, and influence or the number of conversions one is able to produce easily become the ends sought in evangelism. But then there is no longer any good reason to practice evangelism well, to practice it *virtuously*. Christians learn quickly that these ends can be realized without virtue and without their own faithfulness; so the ethics of evangelism degenerate into a crass exercise in doing whatever it takes to achieve those goods and to convert others to Christianity. Christianity is a movement that for the better part of two millennia has been enamored by its own "success." That success, however, and the orientation toward production and results that both fuels and is fueled by it, may well be the biggest obstacle to Christian evangelism practiced well and to a recovery of evangelism as virtuous witness. Perhaps it is time to reconsider the ethics of evangelism.

The Ethics of Evangelism

As right as it strikes me to describe the approach of this book as an "ethics of evangelism," I acknowledge that this way of talking is not a common one and that its two central terms—*ethics* and *evangelism*—do not often intersect. In the first place, questions about the relation of ethics and evangelism typically surface only when considering the questionable tactics of high-pressure evangelistic groups and cults or the moral failures of high-profile evangelists such as Jim Bakker, Jimmy Swaggart, or Jim Jones (apparently we should be wary of evangelists named Jim). Indeed, one of the reasons that Billy Graham earned such wide respect and admiration during his lifetime, even among progressive Christians who reject the content of his evangelism, is the way he managed over almost seventy years of very public ministry to avoid being implicated in sexual or economic misconduct. In our time, and given a documented rise in clergy mistrust, it is striking that an evangelist, of all persons, would have been repeatedly identified in public polling as among the top ten "most admired" persons of the twentieth century.[2] Also, his name was not Jim, so he had that going for him.

One reason, then, why ethics and evangelism do not often intersect in our thinking may be a general perception that they intersect so little in practice. And here we need not confine ourselves only to the shyster television preacher or traveling evangelist—the kind of reprobate portrayed in the Sinclair Lewis novel *Elmer Gantry* or the 1992 film *Leap of Faith*, starring Steve Martin. The history of evangelism is intertwined with stories of imperial conquest, colonialism, forced conversions, and tactics that have come to be known as "scam-vangelism." It is not difficult to understand why the practice of evangelism is ethically suspect, especially in the context of religious pluralism where it is widely perceived as an arrogant attempt to foist one group's religious commitments on others and a manipulative effort to get others to believe and act like the religious group.

2. For example, see the CNN/USA Today Gallup poll conducted in 1999 in which Graham was ranked seventh, with 26 percent of Americans naming him as "one of the people of the century I admire most": http://www.gallup.com/poll/3367/mother -teresa-voted-american-people-most-admired-person-century.aspx.

But a second reason why evangelism and ethics do not often intersect is that the two are widely construed as being focused on very different matters—evangelism on spiritual or other-worldly affairs and ethics on the here and now, on this-worldly concerns of the body, society, economics, and politics. When I attended seminary many years ago, it was almost as if you needed to make a choice between evangelism or social ethics in determining what group you were part of, who your friends were, or with which professors you most closely identified. Those primarily interested in evangelism were typically not part of the ethics or social justice crowd, and those passionate about social ethics disdained the practice of evangelism. Things may have changed, but I doubt if they have changed much. The field of Christian ethics is generally understood to be a field of study preoccupied with such matters as economic and racial justice, sexuality, war, and climate change. Christian ethicists do not always give close attention to core church practices like worship, preaching, evangelism, or religious education. The flip side is that those who study or teach these ecclesial practices don't often think of what they do as an exercise in Christian ethics. Christians might talk about a "theology of evangelism." But an "ethics of evangelism" is not a phrase heard very often, if ever.

Of course, those studying for ministry may find themselves contemplating the relationship between ethics and church life in the form of something called "pastoral ethics," in which they are asked to consider matters of professional conduct, authority, and boundaries in pastoral caregiving. But for the most part, we are not accustomed to thinking *ethically* about most of our core church practices. It would be hard to imagine, for example, members of a congregation complaining to their pastor that they wanted more ethical worship or more ethical preaching. They might well ask that the subject matter of preaching focus on ethical issues. But they are not likely to be concerned that preaching be carried out more ethically. And when it comes to activities like prayer, hospitality, forgiveness, healing, worship, the Lord's Supper, or baptism, little attention has been given to imagining what an ethical framework for reflecting on such important practices would even amount to.[3]

An Ecclesial Ethics

Part of the problem here is a binary between personal ethics and social ethics that is at least partially related to the distinctively modern separation of the personal from the social and the public from the private. While personal ethics might focus on individual decisions related to behaviors such as lying, sexual immorality, substance abuse, gambling, or stealing, social ethics is usually aimed at more systemic issues of injustice, racism, poverty, international relations, war, climate change, and so on. Missing from this binary is an *ecclesial* ethics. In this ethics the church is the logically prior reality from within which Christians understand both the personal and the social and according to which the ordinary practices of the church *are* our ethics. The language of "personal" or "social" need not disappear when thinking about ethics, but they both derive from and find their orientation within our life together as Christ's body. As Stanley Hauerwas says, "The notion that one can distinguish between personal and social ethics distorts the nature of Christian convictions, for Christians refuse to admit that 'personal' morality is less a community concern than questions of justice, and so on" (2001, 372). Thankfully, the past few decades have witnessed the recovery of an ecclesial ethics, and I understand my own work as an attempt to contribute to its further development and recovery.[4]

One chief consequence of framing evangelism within an ecclesial ethics is that the church as the body of Christ rather than some

3. A helpful exception to this is the 1997 World Council of Churches (WCC) Faith and Order Commission document, "Becoming a Christian: The Ecumenical Implications of Our Common Baptism" (Faverges, France, January 17–24). The document includes sections on "Baptism and Ethics" and "Christian Ethics as Baptismal Ethics."

4. For a helpful introduction to ecclesial ethics, see Wells and Quash 2010, 180–206. The authors rightly suggest that the writings of John Howard Yoder, Stanley Hauerwas, Alisdair MacIntyre, and John Milbank, as different as they are from one another, are good examples of ecclesial ethics.

other social body provides the primary formation and habitus for the practice of evangelism. This does not mean that contextualization within other social bodies or forms of culture is irrelevant or an afterthought, or that the church as a social body is either a watertight alternative to other social bodies or an insulated bubble in their midst. But it does mean that the patterns of our faithfulness in any context derive from an ecclesial social imagination that is nurtured and passed along by distinctive stories, practices, and exemplars by which we learn what it means to be a people. Contextualization that grows out of an ecclesial imagination is no exact science, but in the following chapters I explore various social contexts in which evangelism is carried out, and I discuss the ethics of evangelism in each context and the difference that an ecclesial imagination makes. In each case, Christians *as a people* attempt to faithfully embody the good news of Jesus Christ in such a way that it can be touched, tasted, and tried on so that it might be taken seriously and then adopted authentically by others or rejected responsibly.

The good news is not something that precedes its own embodiment so that it is a matter of getting the news right to begin with and then dropping it into this or that situation appropriately "contextualized." Rather, the good news becomes good news precisely as a people embody that gift materially in concrete ways. The challenge for Christians is to bear witness to the good news in ways that make it a present and habitable possibility for others, without contradicting that good news in the very act of offering it—that is, without becoming competitors for space in the world and, as Williams says, "part of its untruth" (6). As Williams puts it,

> The challenge remains, to re-imagine what it is for God to speak to us *as* God—not as a version of whatever makes us feel secure and appears more attractive than other familiar kinds of security. For if our talk about God is a religious version of talk about human safety, the paradox is that it will fail to say anything at all about

salvation. It will not have anything to do with what is decisively and absolutely *not* the way of this world. (15)

Evangelism and Context

A 1967 report of the World Council of Churches titled "The Church for Others" famously said that "the world provides the agenda" for a church that is truly missionary (20). The report called on the church in an increasingly secularized world to look outside of itself to find signs of God's work and Christ's transforming presence in the world, rather than perpetuating a debilitating ecclesiocentrism that turns the church inward and leads it to forget its calling and purpose. But if it can truly be said that the world sets the agenda for the church, this can never mean that the good news turns out to be little more than what persons in a particular context desire or what they might take to be good news on the terms and conditions of the context itself. The good news instead presents its own possibilities, which may very well appear remarkable if not impossible within a particular context. Where the only possibilities might appear to be vengeance, scarcity, fear, suspicion, division, and competition, the good news points to abundance, sharing, reconciliation, and forgiveness. Evangelism is a subversive practice precisely insofar as it is enacted and embodied in the everyday and material practices of a people who see these remarkable new possibilities and refuse to play by the rules of their culture or to buy in to the political, cultural, and economic assumptions of their time. Evangelism is subversive because, in inviting the world to come and see the newness of which it is but a foretaste, the church calls attention to a contrasting identity that is possible in Christ and to what the world (and indeed the church) might become.

Faithful, Embodied Evangelism

At the end of the day, ethics and evangelism are inseparable because the corporate pattern of life we have been given by Christ and into which we are formed as his body is both the medium and the exemplification of the salvation God is offering the world. In other words, our corporate life together as a church does not merely make us more credible witnesses of *the way* we are offering the world; rather, our corporate life together as a church *is* that very way, and this makes our corporate ethics constitutive of evangelistic practice. For an ecclesial ethics, then, the practice of evangelism as the faithful and embodied offer of good news is first and foremost grounded in the habits, disciplines, stories, practices, gestures, and social patterns by which our lives are lived and ordered together as the body of Christ before a watching world. And make no mistake: the world *is* watching. The question is whether we will give the world anything to see. Ethics *is* evangelism.

The good news heralded by the church is that in Christ salvation is now possible in the form of a new way of life. This salvation is not an experience to be passively received or a set of propositions to be assented to. It really is a *way* to be embarked upon, a *way* we forgive each other's sins, a *way* we love and include those who are different from us, a *way* we welcome the poor, a *way* we love our enemies, a *way* we bind up those who are brokenhearted or have suffered loss, a *way* we cancel debts, and a *way* the world's hierarchies are turned upside down in Christlike patterns of fellowship.

Evangelism and Pluralism

One recurring theme throughout the chapters of this book is pluralism. That should not be a surprise, since pluralism pervades the world within which Christians are called to bear witness. And for no Christian practice is pluralism more of a challenge than the practice of evangelism. Evangelism is criticized by both Christians and non-Christians for being associated with attitudes of belligerence and superiority and for being a barrier to mutual understanding and dialogue, especially across interfaith boundaries. After all, it's pretty difficult to listen to another person's religious views honestly and openly when you're attempting to convert them to your own.

It would be better to say that a recurring theme is *pluralisms*, for there are many types of pluralism. Pluralism is not the same thing as plurality. While there may be a plurality of religions, races, or ethnicities, pluralism is *the story we tell about plurality*—the way we construct its meaning, evaluate it, and habituate our practices, institutions, and social patterns within plurality. The fact that we use the single word "religion," for example, to refer to a variety of different phenomena as diverse as Christianity, Buddhism, or civil religion is already an implicit form of pluralism embedded in our vocabulary. We think we have identified common features that unite all these phenomena so that a single word can be applied to each of them equally. In fact, this very example illustrates that pluralisms are really about unities—about how we are to comprehensively comprehend and make sense of the many.

The way unities are imposed on plurality is a complex work of social imagination across time with great consequence for evangelism. As works of imagination (whether implicit or highly theorized), pluralisms set the conditions for how we think about the good news in particular contexts. Indeed, pluralisms can constrict Christian witness so that it can only be imagined on the terms of those pluralisms. Consider, for example, a group of Christians who would like to convert Buddhists to Christianity. The evangelizing Christians in this example are likely operating under the assumption that Buddhism and Christianity are two species of the same genus (religion) and, moreover, that the two are in competition with one another so that the adherents of the one need to be converted to the other. In other words, the evangelists are working out of a particular pluralistic social imagination that both sustains and is sustained by a story about how to understand the plurality they have encountered.

Imagine now a very different group of Christians who oppose evangelistic attempts to convert Buddhists to Christianity and who ground their opposition in the belief that both religions are valid, perhaps even complementary, so that attempting to convert one to the other is wrongheaded and disrespectful. While this second group of Christians are typically called "pluralists," both groups of Christians might well be operating within the same pluralistic framework—one in which Buddhism and Christianity are both "religions" and therefore examples of the same kind of thing. Each group accepts a unity that has been imposed onto the plurality encountered and expressed in their common use of the word "religion" to refer to both phenomena. The fact that they diverge in their assessment of whether the two religions are contradictory or complementary may disguise but ultimately cannot eliminate their mutual starting point: that both phenomena are specimens of the same kind of umbrella phenomenon, that is, "religion." Both groups, we might say, operate from a shared pluralistic social imagination, even though their responses differ from one another.

Throughout this book, I do not accept the pluralisms that present themselves to us in our time as an inevitability, a necessity, a given. Things do not have to be as they are. Pluralisms emerge historically within particular contexts and institutions such as universities, the marketplace, or the military and for particular ideological or pragmatic purposes. They are constructed, have locations, and are produced. For that reason it is possible to speak of *post*pluralism contexts and to use the phrase "evangelism *after* pluralism"—not as if pluralisms were a thing of the past but rather as a way of considering what it means to live and think in the wake of their ideals, possibilities, and prescriptions (cf. Bender and Klassen 2010). Precisely because pluralisms are works of social imagination, they render possible some ways of thinking and acting while other ways remain impossible—or rather *unimaginable*.

An Evangelistic Imagination

In this book, I consider the extent to which pluralisms constrict the Christian evangelistic imagination in at least three ways. First, they represent hegemonic impositions of unity onto plurality that eclipse difference and diminish the importance of and respect for those who have been rendered "other." Second, the kinds of unity they impose force us into competitive modes of comparison and judgment, leading Christians to think we must secure a space in the world for the good news, which largely ends up distorting the good news. Third, prevailing pluralisms distract us from grasping how the powerful unities of empire, nation, and market capture our allegiances, captivate our imaginations, and cultivate vices that undercut and erode the Christian life, not to mention our capacity for bearing faithful witness to the good news.

In the United States, for example, civil religion as an amalgam of patriotism, militarism, and capitalism may be far more relevant as a contrast to Christianity than is Buddhism or Islam. But standard accounts of pluralism obscure this. It would be rare to find a textbook or a class syllabus on world religions that includes "civil religion," despite the fact that, at least in the United States, civil religion may well boast the most adherents. Those who are hell-bent (Matt. 23:15) on converting Buddhists, Muslims, and Hindus to Christianity likely neglect their largest competitor—nationalism, or civil religion—precisely because *they* are *us*. But the prevailing pluralistic social imagination prevents us from seeing this.

The Cultural Contexts of Pluralism

In the following chapters, my concern with pluralism is not, for the most part, focused on the typical and rather abstract questions about the uniqueness, unsurpassability, or finality of Christ, the nature of salvation, or the status of religious truth claims, though these questions all have their place (chapter 8 addresses them to some degree). Instead I attempt to explore how pluralisms are narrated and constructed in three particular cultural contexts: empire, the nation-state (and its military), and consumer culture. The second of these is primarily concerned with the particular case of the United States, though I trust that case has relevance for other contexts, especially insofar as the US version of pluralism enshrines Enlightenment notions about freedom, rights, and the individual that characterize other nations and societies throughout the world. In each case, I explore how these pluralisms habituate the practice of evangelism and how, thus habituated, evangelism becomes an attempt to compete for space in the world, thereby distorting it as a Christian practice.

The problem does not lie with the presence of religious diversity, which Christians need neither fear nor fight. Rather, in all three contexts, a unity is imposed on plurality that possesses an extraordinary capacity for shaping the Christian social imagination and thereby habituating evangelistic practice in ways that are essentially competitive. In each case, I trace how the good news is distorted as a competitor for space in the world—"part of its untruth," as Williams says. But my ultimate hope is to identify a counterimagination that habituates the practice of evangelism in rather different directions and refuses the temptation to secure a space in the world for the good news. Within that alternative imagination, evangelism is the noncompetitive practice of bearing faithful and embodied witness in a particular context rather than an attempt to produce converts by first safeguarding the credibility or helpfulness of the good news. Shaped ecclesially through distinctive social practices, evangelism is the offer of beauty rather than an exercise in positioning the good news within a crowded marketplace in an attempt to fight off the competition.

2

On Ethics, Evangelism, and Proselytism

In 2011, a book with the title *The Ethics of Evangelism* appeared, written by Elmer Thiessen. In his book, Thiessen attempts a defense of proselytization, seeing no need to distinguish between the terms "evangelism" and "proselytization," which are for him synonymous. Though the book's title uses the term "evangelism," the book itself rarely mentions the word and consistently focuses on proselytizing instead. While there is no universally shared agreement on how the two terms differ, I oppose conflating these terms, and it may be helpful toward the beginning of this book to distinguish my approach from Thiessen's, especially given the fact that we both see ourselves as contributing to an "ethics of evangelism."

Defining Evangelism and Proselytism

According to Thiessen, proselytism (and evangelism, since for him they are synonymous) can be defined as "seeking to bring about a religious conversion in another" (2011, 9). Thiessen recognizes that the dimension of agency in this definition is slippery: "Sometimes the lifestyle of a person can lead another to inquire about that person's religious faith, eventually leading to a conversion. Does proselytizing occur in this case? Well, in some sense, yes. Surely covert proselytizing is still an instance of proselytizing. Proselytizing can be intentional or unintentional, direct or indirect, and overt or covert" (10).

While proselytizing can be explicit or intentional, Thiessen believes that in its "full" sense, proselytizing must involve some "explicit verbal communication that is intended to lead someone to convert" (11). It is this narrower definition that he defends in his book and that he unfortunately equates with evangelism more generally.

It is no surprise that proselytizers would feel the need to defend their practice in our time, especially in pluralistic contexts where proselytization is under fire. Social service and health service agencies have attempted to put strict limits on the practice of proselytizing by their employees; military chaplains have covenanted not to engage in it; colleges, universities, and schools in the United States restrict it; and governments around the world seek to prohibit it, especially when practiced by evangelicals whom they see as disguising their proselytizing activity with the cover of humanitarian aid. Thiessen is keenly aware that the term "proselytize" has a largely pejorative connotation, but he seeks to use the term in a more neutral way so that he can show how there are both ethical and unethical ways to practice proselytism. The attempt to convert others *can* be ethical, claims Thiessen, and his project is one of justifying its practice against objections. At its core, his book is about the ethics of persuasion.

The Ethics of Proselytism

One might well agree with Thiessen that, in and of itself, proselytization—the attempt to convert others to one's views, philosophy, political outlook, or religious faith—is not necessarily unethical. There are ethical and unethical ways to sell any product, change someone's mind, persuade another person, or subscribe followers. But there are also good reasons not to conflate evangelism with proselytization or to understand evangelism as an attempt to secure converts. In this chapter, and indeed throughout the entire book, I offer a very different understanding of evangelism so that the reader can see the alternatives alongside each other.

I argue that rather than an attempt to secure converts, the task of evangelism is instead to bear faithful witness to the good news as the people of God in a particular context and in such a way that it can be taken seriously and imagined as an authentic possibility for one's life and for the world. To evangelize is to bear witness to beauty, so that the logic of evangelism is the logic of faithfulness, witness, exemplification, and embodiment rather than the logic of production, competition, or winning.

Conversion versus Faithful Witness

In contrast to Thiessen, I argue that the practice of evangelism is not guided by the aim of conversion, where conversion is conceived of as a good external to that practice and something to be secured through various tactics (even if one might show how those tactics are ethical). It is instead guided by the aim of faithful witness. The ethics of evangelism is concerned more with the character and beauty of our witness than whether that witness yields "results" measured in terms of conversions. The ethics of evangelism, therefore, has nothing to do with whether our attempts to produce conversions are carried out ethically or unethically, since evangelism is not an attempt to produce conversions in the first place. Rather, our evangelism *is* our ethics, and ethics is just a way of talking about "the shape of our faithfulness" (Yoder 1997, 38).

On this view, another person's rejection of the good news, or of a Christian's witness to that good news, cannot be construed as failure for Christians, especially considering the fact that the good news may well come across as bad news for some, at least at

first. Rejection does not count against the truthfulness or fidelity
of Christian witness any more than acceptance of that witness
counts for it. Clarity, accessibility, authenticity, and faithfulness
are the cardinal features of evangelism practiced well, not success
in acquiring adherents or producing church growth. For these
reasons, consequentialist approaches to ethics where the end justifies the means should be subordinated to something like a virtue
ethics where the end is internal to the means—where virtuous
action is its own end. This also has implications for the practice
of evangelism in the context of pluralism, where evangelism is
easily transformed into a competitive practice. When evangelism
is conflated with proselytization, understood by Thiessen as the
attempt to convert others, it is already derailed as a practice by
being aimed at goods external to it, oriented as a competition,
and subject to a logic of production that is foreign to it.

Comparing Proselytization and Marketing

Thiessen frequently compares Christian proselytization to com-
mercial advertising or marketing, and he is surely correct that what
those practices attempt is likewise aimed at bringing about conversion (15). He believes it is disingenuous for persons to criticize
proselytizing efforts on the part of Christians when they have no
problem with the practice in the realm of the secular. For Thiessen, what matters is that proselytizing be carried out ethically in
both arenas. He concludes that "these other forms of proselytizing
might not be that far removed from religious proselytizing" (17),
and though he cautions at the outset of his book that his intent is
not to defend religious proselytizing merely on the grounds that
advertising and marketing are widely accepted, the similarity he
establishes between the two is telling. Indeed, my critique of his
conflation of evangelism with proselytizing is that evangelism is
largely habituated by a thoroughgoing marketing orientation.
Once one accepts the notion that evangelism is an attempt to

convert others, what matters most is how one can best achieve that end; the ethics of evangelism becomes the ethics of utility and production.

Thiessen is surely correct that many of the criticisms of proselytizing could also be made of attempts at persuasion in other arenas of life (proselytizers should keep their convictions to themselves; proselytizers are arrogant and intolerant; proselytizers lack sufficiently rational arguments for their claims). At the same time, I find it hard to agree with Thiessen that "we must be careful not to demand more in the area of religious proselytizing than we do in other areas where proselytizing occurs" (76). Surely the stakes are higher in the case of evangelism or religious proselytizing. Or at least I'd like to believe that bearing witness to the good news about what is ultimately the case in the world and how we therefore ought to live our lives is of an order different from which brand of toothpaste we should use.

One of the criticisms that Thiessen defends against is the accusation that proselytizing is inherently coercive and violates personal freedom and integrity. As Thiessen admits, the history of religions and cults is full of examples of forced conversions, brainwashing, missionary colonialism, offering material inducements in exchange for conversion, and the use of emotional and psychological pressure, such as the exploitation of situations of weakness, loneliness, or need in order to secure conversions. Again, Thiessen asks only that we be consistent in evaluating proselytizing and other forms of propagandizing, advertising, and converting. He has no problem demonstrating that these ethically suspicious means are also found widely in the domains of education, politics, and marketing more generally.

One significant and stark difference between Thiessen's approach to the ethics of evangelism and the ecclesial ethics for which I argue is the basis for his ethical assessment of proselytization. I think it important to articulate that difference up front. Thiessen can cite many violations of human freedom and dignity in the service of proselytization, admitting that "immoral proselytizing does occur, quite frequently, in fact" (42). That does not mean, however, that proselytizing is intrinsically immoral. Thiessen wants to defend the ethics of proselytizing on the basis of his faith in what he takes to be "an objective and universal morality" that both believers and nonbelievers share (37). While Christians might well appeal to a doctrine such as our creation in the image of God as the foundation for the kind of universal human respect and dignity that should characterize our efforts to convert others, Thiessen is more interested in finding moral common ground shared by both Christians and non-Christians. Says Thiessen, "I believe there are a few broad and basic ethical principles, or ideals of virtue, that are shared by all rational human beings concerned about the good life" (37). On the basis of a universal ethics, we can agree, for example, that "compulsion in proselytizing is always wrong" because it violates "the principle of freedom, so essential to the dignity of persons" (40). He continues: "Proselytizing that dehumanizes the person is simply wrong. Using force and violence to convert someone is wrong. Proselytizing that expresses itself in hostility and malice is morally wrong. Dishonesty and duplicity about evangelistic intentions is wrong. Selfishness as a primary motivation to proselytization is wrong" (43).

Thiessen feels no need to justify such claims or to identify their theoretical source, despite the fact that centuries of religious proselytizing, including the better part of Christian history, have relied on the acceptability of force in order to achieve the conversion and correction of nonbelievers. He remarks, "Surely these are values that all decent, caring, and reasonable human beings accept" (43). But these are not in fact universal values that all clear-thinking and caring persons have accepted across time. On the contrary (and as Thiessen makes abundantly clear), in relying on a supposedly universal moral intuition possessed by his readers, the source of his ethical reasoning is actually the tradition of pragmatic liberalism and moral foundationalism, beginning with the Kantian notion of universal ethical demands to which all are obliged. This tradition also includes a Rawlsian framework of "overlapping consensus" that provides a common core for ethical reasoning and is based on the confidence that we live in the same world, have the same access to the same data, and share roughly the same human nature (48). To be sure, Thiessen nods to the natural law tradition as a confirming theological source for this universal moral sense, but it is remarkable to find an evangelical Christian so transparent about the philosophical and moral liberalism that undergirds the practice of proselytizing, which usually goes unnamed. Thiessen helps us see how a conservative approach to ethics and evangelism can be liberal (in the classical sense of that word) through and through.

Universal Moral Imperatives

Augustine is an interesting example in this regard. Thiessen is not unaware of the problem posed by Augustine's endorsement of coercion in evangelism for his argument about the universality of moral imperatives. In *A Treatise Concerning the Correction of the Donatists* (ca. 417), Augustine argues that it is best to draw persons to the worship of God positively, through teaching rather than through "fear of punishment of pain." But it is wrong, he suggests, to conclude that those who do not accept that teaching should simply be left to their ways. On the contrary, in most cases, people must be "corrected by fear." Augustine goes on to say:

> Why, therefore, should not the Church use force in compelling
> [its lost children] to return, if the lost [children] compelled others
> to their destruction? Although even [persons] who have not been
> compelled, but only led astray, are received by their loving mother
> with more affection if they are recalled to her bosom through the
> enforcement of terrible but salutary laws, and are the objects of far
> more deep congratulation than those whom she had never lost. Is
> it not a part of the care of the shepherd, when any sheep have left
> the flock, even though not violently forced away, but led astray by

tender words and coaxing blandishments, to bring them back to
the fold of his master when he has found them, by the fear, or even
the pain of the whip? (1887, §6:21, 23; *NPNF*[1] 4:23)

Augustine's pragmatism leads him to have no problem with
relying on imperial force to achieve what he takes to be Christian
ends (perhaps Thiessen would simply deny that Augustine was
a "decent, caring, and reasonable human being"). Rather than
simply writing Augustine off as unethical by definition based on
the universal consensus Thiessen imagines to be the case, Thiessen
concludes that "Augustine, the crusaders, and Pope Innocent III,
should have known better. Compulsion in proselytizing is always
wrong" (40). My point in raising this issue is not to justify Augustine or the crusaders in using coercive force. Far from it. Nor
do I intend to close the quest for resolving differences through the
kind of dialogue and cooperation by which humans, regardless of
religious convictions, might reach consensus in seeking a better
world. It is to insist, rather, that moral reasoning always begins
from within some tradition of values, stories, practices, and beliefs (and quite often from within communities that are bearers
of those traditions) rather than starting from an allegedly neutral
foundation consisting of "moral powers" and "certain fundamental intuitive ideas" shared by all (Thiessen, 48, quoting Rawls).

The Way of Christ

In contrast to Thiessen and the moral traditions to which he is
indebted, the approach of an ecclesial ethics begins instead with
the distinctiveness of Jesus Christ and his way and the particularity of a people called and empowered to give themselves over to
that way. Christians can certainly extrapolate from the ethics of
this unprecedented peoplehood to invite non-Christians to live
in what they understand to be less violent, more egalitarian, and
more just ways. Indeed, Christians can learn from non-Christians

at every point. But for Christians, peace, equality, and justice are ultimately not derived from foundations in reason and experience (allegedly) shared by all humans. Rather, these have been revealed in the story of the people of God and in the life, death, and resurrection of their messiah, Jesus Christ, into whose body they are being formed.

To identify the ethics of evangelism as an ecclesial ethics derived from a particular story (thus narratival in its logic) and dependent on the formation of a particular community (thus a kind of communitarian "virtue" ethics) is to reject the notion that the ethics of evangelism can be tested, first, by *generalizability* or, second, by *utility* in producing certain ends (conversions, church growth). As to the first, far from being generalizable in the sense that we should not act in any way that we would not expect of everyone, a Christian ethics presupposes that something new and extraordinary has been made possible in the person of Christ, the presence and power of the Holy Spirit, and the redeemed fellowship of the people called the church. We should expect something of Christians that we do not expect of non-Christians. As to the second (utility), Thiessen himself rejects a utilitarian ethical framework in evaluating proselytization, recognizing that such approaches can end up justifying immoral behavior since the end justifies the means.[1] One of the problems with Thiessen's argument, however, is that once evangelism has been defined in terms of a logic of production as "proselytization" with its primary aim understood as securing results in terms of converts, it is virtually impossible for those who practice evangelism (or proselytism) not to slip into precisely this type of consequentialist thinking, especially when evaluating their practice.

It is telling that Thiessen talks little about the character of the proselytizer, the church as the body of Christ, or the Christian's

---

1. As Thiessen says, "If it could be shown that the overall consequences of coercive proselytizing are good, then according to utilitarianism, coercive proselytizing would be justified" (117).

ecclesial formation—or about the nature of salvation, for that
matter. While he says nothing explicit about these, his argument
implies an individualistic notion of salvation as a private, personal
relationship with Jesus fundamentally centered on the free agency,
decision, and self-determining act of the convert's will (167). The
proselytizer's character might well prove important in exerting
persuasive force that could lead the potential convert to a decision,
but that is largely a matter of utility. The ethics of evangelism
is, for Thiessen, the ethics of production and persuasion, not
the ethics of faithful witness. The differences between a witness-
oriented evangelism, such as I am proposing, and a results-oriented
evangelism are momentous. The ethics of evangelism, so I argue,
is an ethics of response, embodiment, and exemplification, not an
ethics of results or extension. It is not that evangelism practiced
faithfully as a form of bearing witness has no purpose, *telos*, or
hope. On the contrary, the church as evangelist seeks to fulfill
the words recorded in Matthew 28:19–20 to "go therefore and
make disciples of all nations, baptizing them in the name of the
Father and of the Son and of the Holy Spirit, and teaching them
to obey everything that I have commanded you." But the church
does this first and foremost by being made "witnesses" (Acts 1:8)
in the power of the Spirit and within a community of those who
have learned that our witness can finally be measured only by its
fidelity to the one to whom it bears witness.

3

Evangelism, Empire, and Rival Citizenships

As I mentioned in the introduction, this book explores the practice of Christian evangelism within a variety of pluralistic contexts. One such context is that of empire. For decades now, theologians, missiologists, and ethicists have attempted to critically engage the reality of empire as an inescapable feature of the world in which Christians live and are called to bear witness. While this is not a new conversation, recent postcolonial theory and the publication of books such as *Empire* (Hardt and Negri 2000) have broadened and intensified the conversation among Christians, who have become increasingly aware of how empire enacts multiple layers of hegemony, which yields a perpetual state of injustice, inequity, and social fragmentation. How are Christians to bear witness to the good news, given the impact of empire on virtually every aspect of our lives and given our complicity as Christians in the economic

This chapter includes and expands portions of Bryan Stone's "The Missional Church and the Missional Empire," *Didache* 13, no. 2 (Winter 2014), http://didache.nazarene .org. Reprinted with permission.

systems, political arrangements, and cultural processes by which empire enacts its seemingly inescapable formations?

Historically speaking, there is no avoiding the association of Christian evangelism with empire. Christianity's early growth throughout Europe, Africa, and Asia is inconceivable apart from imperial edicts, trade routes, and other economic and political structures. The subsequent spread of Christianity around the globe was likewise dependent on imperial infrastructure and ambition. Whether in the Roman Empire, the Ottoman Empire, the British Empire, the Chinese Empire, or the American Empire (to name but a few), Christian witness has always been carried out in the context of empire. It makes a great deal of difference, however, whether that witness is carried out at the fringes and on the underside of empire by a church of martyrs persecuted and marginalized by that empire or whether it is carried out by a church that has assumed the role of chaplain to the empire, succeeding where the empire succeeds and expanding where the empire expands. Martyrdom and chaplaincy, in fact, turn out to be two important and contrasting postures, practices, discourses, and sets of imagination that the church has assumed toward empire. And insofar as they represent radically different ways of relating church to empire, they structure Christian evangelism in dramatically different ways.

The Expansion of Empire

The word "empire" has a largely negative connotation today, especially for those of us who grew up on *Star Wars* films where the force for good was mythologized as resistance against "the empire." But there have always been Christians who saw expansion of empire in positive terms as God-ordained, as God-blessed, as something beneficial and benevolent, and as bringing peace, education, order, and civilization to the world, especially to those persons considered "primitive" or "underdeveloped" and whose lot in life could only be improved with the blessings bestowed by more advanced powers. The presumptions of superiority and exceptionalism are often behind these rationalizations and have long provided justification for Christians to sign on as chaplains of the empire and to support violence in the service of "making the world a safer place" (cf. Sugirtharajah 2004, 26).

Beyond viewing empire as good for the world, Christians have also viewed empire as good for the church and for the gospel. After all, in the fourth century when the empire became officially Christian, the persecution of Christians ceased (Christians would now do the persecuting). It also enabled the relatively rapid spread of Christianity to far-flung corners of the world through an imperial unity imposed on existent plurality by means of roads, language, and political and economic order. By currying imperial favor, traveling aboard imperial ships to the new world, and aiding imperial efforts at colonizing other civilizations, Christians found that their evangelistic efforts profited immensely.

Playing Chaplain to the Empire

Not quite three hundred years ago, however, an Anglican priest named John Wesley described Christian chaplaincy to the empire as "the fall" of the church. "Persecution," said Wesley, "never could give any lasting wound to genuine Christianity. But . . . the grand blow which was struck at the very root of that humble, gentle, patient love, which is the fulfilling of the Christian law, the whole essence of true religion, was struck in the fourth century by Constantine the Great, when he called himself a Christian, and poured in a flood of riches, honours, and power upon the Christians, more especially upon the clergy" (1984, 2:462–63). Thus empire made the task of evangelism easier for Christians—and to follow Wesley's train of thought, the church has been paying the price ever since.

While it is inaccurate to imagine with Wesley a pristine early church in comparison with which everything after the third century was a decline, there are important and marked differences

between the character of the church's pre-Christendom witness
and the character of its witness once allied with imperial power.
Prior to its role as chaplain of the empire, the church's visible
deviance was intrinsic to its witness, as the lives and deaths of
its martyrs attested. Its confession that Jesus is Lord was at the
same time a political confession—Caesar is not Lord. The church
"evangelized" by forgiving enemies, welcoming the stranger, sharing bread with the poor, and refusing to fight imperial wars or
engage in imperial entertainments. Its corporate life together in
the world *was* its offer to the world of a new creation. Its ethics
was its evangelism. Having made peace with the empire, however,
the church's social imagination began to shift in significant ways.

John Howard Yoder points out what was most striking about
the transition from a pre-Constantinian church to a Constantin-
ian church: "[It] is not that Christians were no longer persecuted
and began to be privileged, nor that emperors built churches and
presided over ecumenical deliberations about the Trinity." Rather,
says Yoder, "what matters is that the two visible realities, church
and world, were fused. There is no longer anything to call 'world';
state, economy, art, rhetoric, superstition, and war have all been
baptized" (1994, 57). This is of course a loss that has had tremen-
dous consequences for Christian mission and evangelism. Baptism,
rather than enacting one's transition from death to newness of life
in Christ through incorporation into his body, would now mark
one's membership in the empire, a very different body.

Distinguishing the Church in Imperial Contexts

A church that has become fused with world (or, more specifi-
cally, with empire) can no longer look to the distinctiveness of its
corporate life in the world as *the form* of its witness—as that which
"proclaims"—and even less can it look to the distinctiveness of
its corporate life as that to which its witness is an invitation. The
church's invitation to others is now reduced to nominal membership
in an institution, to the guarantee of salvation as afterlife, or, under

the conditions of modernity, to a private, interior, and hyperspiritualized relationship with God. Whatever the case, the church's project becomes compatible (if not identical) with the empire's project, and we have, in effect, a situation of chaplaincy that has characterized the church's practice of evangelism for much of its history.

In so identifying itself with empire through an ethics of chaplaincy, the church does far more than bless, pray for, sing songs about, or wave the flag of the empire as its own. The church now allows itself to be recruited by the empire for killing those that the empire counts as its enemies, serving and benefiting from the empire's economic conquests, and inevitably imagining its own corporate life together on terms set for it by the empire. Empire is seductive and its "blessings" hard to resist. To the extent that the practice of evangelism adopts its logic and is habituated into its social imagination, empire extends the reach of the church and secures "results."

Those results are a mixed blessing, however, and one could even make the case that in some contexts empire prevented the spread of Christianity. Lamin Sanneh, for example, has traced the impressive growth of Christianity in postcolonial contexts and suggests, "Perhaps colonialism was an obstacle to the growth of Christianity, so that when colonialism ended it removed a stumbling block" (2003, 10). The question for practicing evangelism in a postcolonial context can no longer be the imperial question of how we can reach more people, grow our churches, or expand our influence. The more fundamental question is whether the church can relearn how to bear public witness on the Spirit's terms rather than the empire's terms, recapturing some of the ancient church's counterimperial deviance while imagining ever new forms of faithfulness.

Empire and the Domestication of the Church

Our present imperial context is complex to say the least. Empire is not always visibly recognized for what it is. Though now, at the beginning of the twenty-first century, many understand the United States to be a global empire, empire is not reducible to a single nation-state, person, or emperor as its agent; it is instead a complex, multilayered, and decentered reality. Empire is a complex invention of social and political imagination over time that embraces complex multinational economic interests and influences an astonishing range of scientific, educational, cultural, and technological dimensions of life. Joerg Rieger, in thinking about empires across history, defines them as "massive concentrations of power that permeate all aspects of life and that cannot be controlled by any one actor alone" (2007, 2). Thus, even if Alexander the Great may be said to have formed an empire and even if the US president presides over one today, empire is always much more than what any one agent is able to create or maintain. Indeed, within our present context, empire has become even more complex and expansive given its relations to the boundary-defying ambitions of global capitalism. We can speak of empire, therefore, as "seek[ing] to extend its control as far as possible; not only geographically, politically, and economically—these factors are commonly recognized—but also intellectually, emotionally, psychologically, spiritually, culturally, and religiously" (2–3).

The Coercive Unity of Empire

A characteristic feature of empire throughout history is its tendency to devalue the particularity of peoples and places in favor of imperial unity. This occurs not only in the realm of cultural practices and patterns but also in the very way we think—in our imperial worldviews, rationalities, and phobias. Empires expand and maintain their power by the homogenization of place through the imposition of a unified and totalizing "order" that erases difference so that one place is the same as another. Thus, whether one is in Jerusalem, Antioch, or Nazareth, all is Rome (Stone 2010, 105–12).

Empires rise and are sustained by their ability to control, whether through more overt forms of physical, economic, or political coercion or through more subtle forms of cultural co-optation. Empires tell stories. And stories have power. Empires also erase difference and suppress alternatives so that the church, by becoming linked to empire, finds its rivals overpowered and the path paved for its evangelistic "success." Such success is often superficial as indigenous values, traditions, practices, and beliefs are retained below the surface, producing hybridized forms of Christianity (imperial Christianity is, of course, also hybridized!). As has often been noted by postcolonial theorists, empires typically allow such arrangements and encourage local adaptations to the larger structures of imperial unity, power, and control. Hardt and Negri describe contemporary empire as "a *decentered* and *deterritorializing* apparatus of rule that progressively incorporates the entire global realm within its open, expanding frontiers. Empire manages hybrid identities, flexible hierarchies, and plural exchanges through modulating networks of exchange" (xiii).

Subjugated Traditions in Empire

The consequences of empire on colonized, enslaved, and obliterated peoples throughout the world are well known. For many colonized countries, the struggle for independence is simultaneously a struggle not only to de-Westernize but also to liberate themselves from Christianity and to reassert indigenous traditions that were originally suppressed but not lost from local memory altogether. These traditions are often an underground well that sustains subjugated peoples and nourishes their resistance to empire across time.

Perhaps it is not surprising, then, that justice-seeking Christians have at times found more in common with subjugated non-Christian traditions than with those forms of Christianity allied with empire. This very dynamic, in fact, already calls into question any simple understanding of religious pluralism as consisting primarily of the relation between major religious traditions. The consequences of empire are hybridizations and contested identities so that clearly distinguishing one religion from another is not always so easy; religious pluralism is frequently much deeper and more complex than appears on the surface or in standard textbook treatments.

The Shape of Evangelism

Because the "conglomerates of power" (Rieger, vii) that we call empires wield such extensive influence, the challenge before us is to interrogate the ways evangelism has been shaped by the expansionist logic of empire and at the same time to detect how Christians have kept from being co-opted by empire—that is, how Christians have refused to compete for space on the empire's terms or within its social imagination. For while it is true that no one escapes the empire's influence completely, it is also true, as Rieger notes, that "empire is never quite able to extend its control absolutely" (3–4). The good news is that Christian witness has not always been overtaken completely by empire and that from the beginning there have always been Christians who understood the church's mission in the world not as a form of chaplaincy to the powers but as a form of obedient and counterimperial witness to the nonviolence of God's reign.

The problem, however, is that it is increasingly difficult to know who and where the emperor is or when we are serving as the emperor's chaplains. It is also true that while it is difficult to resist a pagan empire, to refuse to fight its wars or worship its gods, it is far more difficult to resist an empire that has come to think of itself as Christian (Cavanaugh 1998, 80). Then too, one difference between fourth-century empire and twenty-first-century empire is that the latter is typically far less interested in securing and defending a single official religious sponsor or chaplain and more adept at domesticating all religions equally as purveyors and administrators of essentially private experiences. Twenty-first-century empire, rather than persecuting religious heretics or minorities (in most cases), can afford to protect religion as a private good by assigning it to a private space protected from public interference while also protecting a pluralistic public against the vagaries and particularities of religion. Religious institutions now become essentially privatized arms of what Rui de Souza Josgrilberg has called "the great global machine" and are dedicated to the administration of a particular set of "spiritual" goods and services: "The global machine incorporates in itself the religious dimension" (2006, 10).

An ironic feature of our present situation is that as religion grows in its public importance around the world, deeply shaping international relations and playing an important role in the formation of social and national identities, religious faith and practice has become increasingly private in the West, constructed as it is within a paradigm of individual consumer choice in which we are taught to respect and keep our "hands off" our neighbor's religious preferences. I write from within the unique context of the United States, where, on one hand, presidential candidates have to present themselves as people of faith (one who claims to be an atheist would not likely get elected at this point in history) while, on the other hand, our candidates must try to convince us that their faith won't actually make any difference to their politics.

As the empire domesticates the church, it similarly domesticates (and thereby de-forms) evangelistic practice by treating salvation and the path to salvation as a private, personal choice, journey, or experience. At the same time, ironically, Christian faith must be commended and validated by "public" (and, therefore, what are alleged to be universal) criteria of rationality or usefulness. Otherwise, evangelistic witness can only be the intrusion of what is "private" where it has no business. The problem, of course, is that if Christian salvation actually names a *way*, then evangelism requires a visibly faithful church that both exhibits and offers this way through public habits, disciplines, and social patterns by which our lives are lived and ordered together. A Christian ethics of evangelism begins by rejecting both the notion that salvation is essentially private as well as the notion that there is out there some wider "public" that we must engage in order to be relevant or credible. Instead, the church is "the public of the Holy Spirit" (Hütter 2000, 158). The way of Jesus is to be lived out before a watching world with or without the support and endorsement of that world.

This de-formation of Christian witness by diminishing the sense of the church itself as a public also diminishes the sense of the church as a politics, and one that is rival to other politics. In other words, by accepting its relegation to the sphere of the private, the church allows its relationship to empire to become depoliticized. As Rieger writes, "One of the odd things about empire in our time is that many people have no sense for the pressures produced by empire and do not perceive empire at work. As a result, there is no context for observing the difference between Christ as Lord and the emperor as Lord. This may explain the otherwise strange attraction to 'purely religious' and depoliticized language. Yet when Christians in a context of empire are unaware of the political implications of their faith, their Christ is likely to be co-opted by empire by default" (44). So Jesus as Lord now becomes compatible with the emperor as Lord. In reality, of course, a depoliticized faith is thoroughly political precisely by virtue of its blind acquiescence to the political status quo.

If contemporary manifestations of empire incorporate—and even nurture—religious institutions as a way of meeting the private spiritual needs of its subjects, they cannot tolerate the kind of material community that might end up threatening their imposed unity or that function as a rival social body or politics in and through which persons are formed into a social imagination other than that of empire. As Cavanaugh has quipped, "Wherever two or three are gathered, there is subversion in their midst" (1998, 38). Yet the church is created and called by the Spirit to be just such a social body with its own distinctive social imagination rooted in the worship of God and in practices and social patterns that are the very shape of its faithfulness.

Empire domesticates religion either by relegating it to the sphere of the private or by preserving a chaplaincy role for it in the public sphere. But when the church is domesticated by empire, it no longer functions as a public in its own right—a social body with the capacity to embody, much less witness to, a new world. The church thus privatized, spiritualized, and depoliticized ends up "helping" the colonized adjust themselves to empire instead of enacting an embodied critique of the system that produced their colonization in the first place. This help might come in the form of pieties and spiritualities or it might come in the form of material and cultural institutions and support, such as schools, hospitals, and social charities. But empire remains intact. When the domesticated church does "go public," it tends to do so within the social imagination of empire, on its terms, and within its discourse.

Salvation as Individualistic Experience

Evangelism under these conditions is carried out in ways that are perfectly compatible with the increasingly hegemonic and far-ranging claims of the empire over our lives. This is especially true when evangelism is aimed at securing salvation construed as a fundamentally private experience, something that only in the past century came to be known as a "personal relationship with Jesus." This private relationship with Jesus is imagined as being neutral with regard to social location, income, race, gender, and politics. At least in theory, the wealthy landowner can sing praises to the Jesus who has "filled [his] heart with gladness" right alongside the impoverished twelve-year-old girl who cuts sugarcane in his fields. The same Jesus who "lives within the heart" of the woman from Oklahoma who just paid six dollars for a pair of jeans at Walmart also stands knocking at the heart of a woman in Bangladesh who made those jeans at the rate of ten pairs per hour and was paid just fourteen cents for the entire hour. Empire will never have a problem with "personal relationships with Jesus" abstracted from bodies both physical and social and thus made compatible with the imperial discipline of bodies in service of the security of the empire and the goods it bestows on its subjects.

If the church in the United States is to recover the practice of evangelism for a post-Christendom world, it must find new ways to reclaim its public witness not merely *in* society but as a new and alternative society. The problem is that those we tend to look to as exemplars of public witness typically operate from the residual assumptions of Christendom about the church's relationship to world and so come to believe that public witness means swinging presidential elections or dominating school boards rather than modeling before the world a new politics of the Spirit that turns the world upside down (Acts 17:6). "In other words, the public witness we do have is too often but a parody of itself, a caricature, and little more than a voting bloc. A voting bloc, however, is not a church. And to the extent that this is the most to which our [public] witness amounts, we will never pose a problem to the aspirations of empire," nor will we represent anything like a challenge to the violence, racism, affluence, and individualism of our culture, having instead become enamored of them all (Stone 2010, 112).

The Problem of Rival Citizenships

Humorist Garrison Keillor once mused about whether the United States should pass a constitutional amendment to take the right to vote away from born-again Christians. He reasoned that they are citizens of heaven, not citizens "here among us in America" (2004). Keillor went on to observe that Scandinavians aren't allowed to vote in our elections. Nor are Canadians, even though they might be perfectly well-informed on the issues. So why should the United States let people vote in its elections who claim their primary citizenship elsewhere?

Though offered in jest, Keillor suggests quite rightly that inevitable political and public consequences come with the claim of citizenship in God's commonwealth. Of course, this assumes that Christians take seriously the material consequences of their citizenship in God's commonwealth, not to mention taking them as primary. Not surprisingly, Keillor singles out "born-again" Christians in this regard, since they often tend to be more vocal in public about their "heavenly" citizenship despite the fact that, as polling in the United States shows year after year, rates of divorce, sexual promiscuity, and racist attitudes among born-again Christians in the United States are little different from those for non-Christians, and in some years rates are several percentage points higher (Sider 2005b, 17–30). Born-again Christians are also more likely than other Christians, or even non-Christians, to support war or military interventions.

But Keillor's jab should apply to all Christians and not just to those who wear the "born-again" label. The apostle Paul says, "Our citizenship is in heaven" (Phil. 3:20), and the author of the Epistle to the Ephesians describes the church as "citizens with the saints and also members of the household of God" (2:19). To be a Christian is to accept citizenship in God's commonwealth as primary rather than citizenship in some other nation or empire, regardless of our place of birth or residence. However, citizenship in God's commonwealth does not mean that other citizenships are rejected altogether. But it does mean those other citizenships are relativized and subordinated to this primary citizenship, which manifests itself in some very material and earthly consequences. Indeed, we should not be surprised to find citizenship in God's commonwealth to be in material conflict with other citizenships. Michael Budde rightly talks about how ecclesial solidarity makes Christians "members of a community broader than the largest nation-state, more pluralistic than any culture in the world, more deeply rooted in the lives of the poor and marginalized than any revolutionary movement, more capable of exemplifying the notion of 'E pluribus unum' [out of many, one] than any empire past, present, or future" (2011, 4). Yet this "membership" too often resembles little more than a brand name.

If it is true that Christians understand themselves to have a citizenship, unity, and solidarity vaster than the largest empire or nation-state, then Budde is also correct that "when Christians kill one another in service to the claims of state, ethnicity, or ideology," this is "the most damning indictment of Christianity in the modern era" and "a scandal to the gospel, a cruel inversion of the unity of the body of Christ, [and] among the most embarrassing charges against contemporary Christianity" (4–5). I would argue that Christians are called to refuse the killing not only of Christians but of all persons. But the deeper point here is that Christians killing Christians (along with the reality that at times this is not even perceived as scandalous) reveals graphically the diminishment, if not loss, of solidarity and unity, which comes with our primary allegiance to and citizenship in the church as a transnational body that nourishes us and forms us into a people who have renounced killing.

The greatest obstacle to evangelism today may be not a lack of missional vitality or creativity in how to attract unchurched people to our churches but rather the reality that Christians tend to identify more with national allegiances than Christian allegiances— "they have been formed more deeply by the narratives, stories, and symbols of nationalism than by the gospel" (Budde, 88). The nation becomes, in effect, the church (Cavanaugh 2011, 104). If that is true, then the ethics of evangelism begins with a renunciation of national identities and citizenships as primary along with a relativizing of national borders that comes with that renunciation. The renunciation of these borders and identities as primary does not mean that they must be renounced altogether (though there may be times when that is true), but Christians with a fully catholic vision of God's concern for all may well find themselves exiled in their own homeland. It would not be inappropriate to think of a post-Christendom ethics of evangelism in the West as an ethics of exile. To be sure, our present exilic situation is far different from Israel's exile in Assyria, since the culture of the West is the creation of Christians and retains visible and important vestiges of Christian chaplaincy to Western cultures, nations, and empires. This leaves Christians with the enormous task of identifying what the good news is as a *way* that we can offer to others without simply reaching for the cultural markers of Christendom.

Catholicity and Commonwealth

Evangelism in our time is an invitation to conversion—but not a conversion from *within* an imperial imagination; rather it is a conversion *from* an imperial imagination to another one altogether. In the body of Christ, the universalizing, imperial claim to space is contested, and as citizens of heaven, the church is called instead to be a space in the world where the commonwealth of God can appear materially, locally, and bodily. The church is catholic, and so it too understands itself in global terms, but Christian catholicity is something quite different from imperial claims to universality. Instead, the church as catholic is a place and a time in which persons are habituated into a transnational and transcultural body—a body that engenders solidarity across social lines rather than offering the rootlessness and placelessness of empire.

Twenty-first-century globalization undoubtedly provides new opportunities for the church to regain its catholicity and to recover its existence as a new and distinct "race" (1 Pet. 2:9) forged in baptism, relativizing all other national or ethnocentric identities. At the same time, one task for a church that understands itself in global terms is to guard against ways both the church and its missional "reach" have come to be shaped by the logic and discourse of empire, especially when empire is intrinsically linked to the ambitions of global capital. When baptism is overly spiritualized and privatized, and our primary loyalties and ties are to a nation or empire, it is no longer the unity of baptism but the unity of global consumption that characterizes our ties to one another.

In contrast to an ethics of chaplaincy that accepts the church's domestication within the space and on the terms that empire has provided us, our primary task is not to find better ways to engage the church more effectively in imperial politics but to be a distinctive politics in the context of empire; not merely to do as well as we can within the economic system presented to us but to be an alternative economics. We need not set out to provoke and subvert, but this we do by modeling Christ's forgiveness, inclusion, and nonviolence. By including the marginalized, by preferring the poor, by refusing to kill our empire's enemies, we not only bear witness to the good news that Jesus is Lord and Caesar is not; we also bear witness to Jesus's subversion of lordship itself and to longstanding patterns of hierarchy, patriarchy, household orderings, and imperial rule. We instead bear witness to an entirely new social imagination rooted in shalom and a new citizenship in the commonwealth of God.

Jesus was not wrong in announcing the arrival of God's reign; the new age has begun, and the church can be—is called and empowered to be—the embodied and corporate witness to that new age and the sign of what is to come. The reign of God, however, is not real because we make it so. It is made visible when, in the midst of oppression, terrorism, and empire, a people take as their first and primary mission to live publicly as citizens of the commonwealth of God, thereby making visible in and with their own bodies the body of Christ.

4

The Ecclesiality of Salvation

Over the last half century, as a response to the church's long history of chaplaincy to empire, some theologies have emphasized God's kingdom and mission as more expansive than the church. Hoping to counteract the inherited ecclesiocentrism of Christendom, they have called for a relativization and subordination of the church's mission to the *missio Dei*. Such ecclesiocentrism not only permitted but also sustained the church's chaplaincy role as the church became preoccupied with its own security, prosperity, and expansion. Though I don't defend ecclesiocentrism and instead affirm that the church must ever move outward in service to the world, we do lose something important when the church is subordinated to mission and instrumentalized in relation to salvation, rendering the church an afterthought or optional altogether. The practice of a postcolonial Christian evangelism begins with a recognition that church and empire are rival "social imaginaries," which, through the complex of practices, habits, relationships, and stories they engender, have the power to script our lives, to discipline our bodies, to structure our social relations, and to habituate us (often unconsciously) into ways of living and acting that come to be understood as not only possible but natural and right (cf. Cavanaugh 2011, 31). To use the word "imaginary" in this way does not mean we are talking about something fantastic or less real. To refer to Christianity and empire as rival social imaginaries is to point to the way each of them is capable of forming us according to broad sets of common assumptions about the way things are and the way things ought to be. A social imaginary is, as Charles Taylor puts it, an "ensemble of imaginings that enable our practices by making sense of them" (2004, 165).

Much is at stake for evangelism regarding whether it is practiced from within the social imaginary of empire, which claims to secure peace through violence, or from within the social imaginary of the ecclesia, for which peace is not something we can secure in the first place. Rather, peace names the path we take when following a nonviolent savior. Each of these social imaginaries offers not only a different "peace" but also a different social formation, entailing a different relationship to violence.

Our present imperial context renders it as important as ever to affirm that Christian salvation has an intrinsically ecclesial dimension and that God's activity in the world (the *missio Dei*) is centrally about calling and forming a Christ-shaped people who embody and thereby proclaim to the world a new humanity—a humanity that stands in contrast to imperial social orderings and formations. As Lesslie Newbigin puts it, "The Church cannot fulfill the Kingdom purpose that is entrusted to it . . . if it sees its role in merely functional terms. The Church is sign, instrument and foretaste of God's reign for that 'place,' that segment of the total fabric of humanity, for which it is responsible—a sign, instrument and foretaste for that place with its particular character" (1989, 138). While the church must be "missional," in an important sense, mission must also be "ecclesial."

Cyprian and the Ecclesiality of Salvation

In the third century, Cyprian of Carthage famously wrote that "outside the church there is no salvation" (1931, 272–73). For

Cyprian, the claim is essentially a tautology. To be "saved" as a Christian is to enter into a distinct form of social existence called the church. The unity of this new social order is marked by bishops who preside over the church, and so the church in Cyprian's time is already coming to take on an institutional form. But the church is not a mediator of salvation, as if salvation were something other than the church itself. To be saved is to be formed into Christ's body. So of course there is no salvation outside that body.

In the centuries after Cyprian, as the church began to absorb the social imagination of empire and to develop more elaborate institutional and hierarchical forms, the claim that "outside the church there is no salvation" came to mean something quite different from what Cyprian meant. Now salvation would be construed as something conferred, guaranteed, and dispensed by the church, which was itself conceived of as a perfect institution. To be sure, Cyprian's images for the church—an ark, a walled garden, a sealed fountain, and so forth—lent themselves to later Christendom interpretations. But Cyprian's was a church that had recently passed through the brutal Decian persecution, and his assertion of the ecclesiality of salvation was formed in that context, on the underside of empire, as a way of marking the distinctive life together that characterized what it means to be the church. His was a church whose politics was rival to empire rather than a church that had become the endorsing arm of an imperial politics. That difference makes all the difference.

In a Christendom context, the church shifted from being the very form that salvation takes to being an institutional mediator, or instrument, of salvation. Within modernity, many Christians would reject the Christendom notion that the church has that sort of power or that it has authority over who is and who is not saved. They rightly reject the ecclesiocentrism presupposed in such a notion. But in modernity the church is no less instrumentalized in relation to salvation. Given modern conceptions of salvation as essentially private and individual, as a commodity to be acquired

in the context of other goods and services, the church becomes a
consumer-oriented vendor of salvation as something helpful and
useful. Salvation is a reward given to those who believe particular
claims or who experience Jesus as their personal savior. And so it
is that in modernity the very individualism from which we need to
be saved comes to shape and define salvation. The church, rather
than being experienced as the remedy to individualism and the very
form that salvation takes, becomes instead a collection of "saved"
individuals. Ironically, as Andrew Davison and Alison Milbank
point out, for early Christians this kind of individualism came
with excommunication, "the ultimate penalty and remedy for of-
fenders" (2010, 57). Even then, it was to last only for a period so
that the sinner would understand the ecclesial shape of salvation.

One of the great tasks of Christianity in the twenty-first century is to recover the ecclesiality of salvation without accepting
the ecclesiocentrism born of Christendom and moving beyond the
individualism of modernity. Salvation then is a way of naming our
life together as Christians, our new peoplehood made possible by
participation in Christ's body. In the words of Karl Barth:

> [The Christian] is not in [the church] in the sense that [he or she]
> might first be a more or less good Christian by [his or her] per-
> sonal choice and calling and on [his or her] own responsibility as
> a lonely hearer of God's Word, and only later, perhaps optionally
> and only at [his or her] own pleasure, [he or she] might take into
> account [his or her] membership in the church. If [he or she] were
> not in the church, [he or she] would not be in Christ. [He or she] is
> elected and called, not to the being and action of a private person
> with a Christian interest, but to be a living member of the living
> community of the living Lord Jesus. (1970, 188)

The point here is not that the church is a useful social instrument
for mediating an otherwise private, individual, and formless salvation to persons but rather that the shape of the salvation we have
been given by God is our transformation from mere *individuals*

into socially constituted *persons* through an incorporation into Christ's body (cf. Zizioulas 1985). As Davison and Milbank write, "Christian redemption is more than the sum of a billion separate and independent reconciliations with God. Reconciliation with God is also reconciliation with one another" (72). In and through the event of reconciliation, the individual becomes redeemed as a person who is genuinely open to others, thereby gaining rather than losing identity and particularity. John Howard Yoder puts it well:

> The political novelty that God brings into the world is a community of those who serve instead of ruling, who suffer instead of inflicting suffering, whose fellowship crosses social lines instead of reinforcing them. This new Christian community in which the walls are broken down not by human idealism or democratic legalism but by the work of Christ is not only a vehicle of the gospel or only a fruit of the gospel; it is the good news. It is not merely the agent of mission or the constituency of a mission agency. This is the mission. (1994, 81)

Caveats Regarding a Counterwitness to Empire

Three caveats are in order before leaving this topic. First, neither missionality nor ecclesiality in and of itself can guarantee a counterwitness to empire, as Christendom teaches us quite clearly. If, for example, God is imagined in patriarchal terms as a heavenly monarch who rules from above and endorses the ruling establishments on earth, the church has likely already acquiesced to empire. Part of the difficulty with thinking about the ecclesial shape of salvation and thus the kind of reimagining of evangelism required along those lines is that the church is so often viewed in Western cultures as a nonprofit organization. As Michael Budde says, "Designating the Church as such—as a voluntary organization of like-minded people who join together in a common interest or pursuit of common tasks—situates the Church as a useful part of the public order, serving the nation by providing goods and services beyond the confines

of Church membership" (2011, 155). Budde goes on to show how
theories of church management and leadership are formed as if
the church were just another kind of service organization, not
altogether unlike a for-profit organization, complete with leaders
who function as executives within management hierarchies.

Second, the ecclesiality of salvation does not mean that Christ
is present only in the church or that Christ belongs solely to the
church as a possession. Cyprian's dictum that there is no salvation
outside the church cannot mean that God's activity and presence
is less than fully cosmic in scope. The church, moreover, is not
the kingdom of God. On the contrary, to affirm the ecclesiality
of salvation means that the individual is not the starting point for
talking about Christian salvation or the Christian life, which is
a "life together," as Dietrich Bonhoeffer so eloquently describes
(1954). An ecclesially shaped mission is a mission fully engaged
in the world, but not on the world's (or the nation's or the empire's) terms.

Third, as Nicholas Healy writes, "The church is sinful and
'worldly,' and the Spirit acts throughout creation; so 'church' and
'world' may often be more prescriptive than descriptive categories"
(2000, 170). Saying that for Christians the shape of salvation is
ecclesial does not claim perfection for the church. On the contrary, confession of sin is a central ritual that defines the church *as*
church (and thus defines its mission). The ethics of evangelism is
an ethics of humility forged in the practice of confession so that
what we offer the world is neither a possession to be given away
nor a static perfection. It is rather a state of dispossession, of not

being in control, of moving outward toward God and others in
gratitude, openness, hope, and prayer.

Reclaiming the Church's Witness

There are plenty of signs today that the chaplaincy of the church
to empire is being rejected, especially by marginalized communities

that have never had any stake in that chaplaincy in the first place. In city after city, one now finds alternative Christian communities comprised of disciples who have covenanted to live visibly and publicly in ways that run counter to prevailing social patterns. Within these deviant Christian bodies, social lines are being crossed rather than reinforced; the poor are being valued; strangers are being welcomed; material goods are being shared; and a refusal to celebrate or participate in imperial violence is being cultivated. The witness of these communities is visible but not always heroic or headline grabbing.

Communities like these suggest that for the church to birth disciples in our current imperial context, it will have to reclaim a public and material witness that understands its primary citizenship as located in God's commonwealth rather than in empire or nation. This can take many forms: an outdoor church in Boston that intentionally welcomes persons without adequate housing, a community of Christians living on the United States–Mexico border that practices hospitality to immigrants, or a "new monastic" community in San Francisco that practices a form of common purse as a way of living out its Christian economic commitments. These communities all violate the imperial boundaries of public and private and the empire's domestication of religion to a private good. As a result, they make visible the body of Christ in and through their own bodies, both personally and corporately, thereby helping us locate the church.

Of course one might argue that locating the church visibly and bodily is not really a problem. Churches seem to be on every street corner. And after all, we now have Google Maps and onboard global positioning systems. Do we really need help locating the church? As most of us know almost instinctively, the church as a community of disciples does not appear in the world simply because there is a sign out front that says "church" or because we happen to encounter tall steeples, bell choirs, and bad coffee. Nor can it be found simply by going to the phone directory and looking under the letter *c*. The church is the Spirit-empowered and Christ-shaped performance of an alternative social imagination in which first are last and last are first, in which strangers are welcomed rather than deported, in which enemies are forgiven rather than persecuted or killed. This social imaginary embodies a new creation in the world, ritualized in baptism, in which all prior social differences, whether given or chosen, are no longer determinative for our relations to one another. Around the table of Christ, the church is the concrete enactment of a time and space that rivals time and space as defined by empire.

5

Evangelism and Pluralism in the Nation-State and Military

In the prior chapters, I argued that empire imposes a unity onto plurality that has long captivated the Christian social imagination and the practice of evangelism. Another context in which pluralism is narrated and constructed in our time—one closely related to empire—is the modern nation-state (a term that conjoins the political notion of a "state" with the cultural-ethnic notion of a "nation"). In this chapter, I focus on the United States and its distinctive form of civil religion that enshrines Enlightenment values of freedom, rights, and the individual in a matrix of patriotism, militarism, and consumerism. Insofar as the Enlightenment values that shape the United States are shared by other nation-states throughout the world, the US context is not entirely unique. And yet the United States has a distinctive history of uniting the features of nation-state with the aspirations of empire.

As with the context of empire, the practice of evangelism is susceptible to being habituated by the pluralistic imagination of modern liberal nation-states and transformed into yet another attempt to compete for space in the world. To demonstrate this, I concentrate on the US military as a microcosm for seeing evangelism in a pluralistic context, as narrated by the nation-state. In some ways, the military is unique because of the intense plurality that it necessarily embraces and because of the particular ways violence, defense, and war-making are related to its reason for being. But if the military context is *unique*, it can also be *illustrative* of how pluralism is constructed more broadly and of the ways civil religion habituates evangelistic practice in our time.

In the context of pluralism fostered by the nation-state and cultivated within a religious and political imagination that is at once individualistic and nationalistic, the practice of evangelism may become entangled in a complex dance of rights and freedoms that are coordinated and defended by the state, which imposes its own salvific unity onto plurality. While evangelism is carried out as a competition for individual souls, rarely does it threaten civil religion with which it often fits hand-in-glove.

Pluralism and the US Military Chaplaincy

The relationship of religious pluralism to the practice of evangelism in the context of the US military is hardly an arbitrary association since evangelism and religious pluralism are so frequently narrated as threats to one another within that context. Military chaplaincy, moreover, has become the turf on which that contest has often played itself out. More so than any other public space of its size and influence, the military is deliberately constructed as a religiously pluralistic environment with considerable attention given to accommodating diverse religious practices as long as that accommodation does not adversely affect military readiness. The military is an extraordinary environment in this regard since, far more than other pluralistic contexts such as public schools, prisons, or hospitals, it brings together people from across the United States and from a variety of backgrounds, and it requires that they depend on one another very closely. This it does, however, under the canopy of the big tent of America's civil religion, in which individual and group religious differences are preserved and protected, as long as they contribute to, or at least do not thwart, the larger projects of the nation-state.

Religious Diversity in the Military

In 2017, the Department of Defense expanded its list of recognized religions to include 221 denominations and faith traditions (including Pagan, Humanist, and Heathen) that are represented among US military personnel and served by chaplains representing those groups (Winston 2017). Since personnel are under no obligation to report their affiliation or preference, it is difficult to gauge precisely the religious diversity in the military. However, Department of Defense data and other recent studies show that the military is about 20 percent Catholic, 11 percent Baptist, 13 percent other Protestant, and 27 percent other Christian, without denominational preference (Kamarck 2016). The remaining 30 percent includes the 28 percent who are reported as having "no religious preference" or as "unknown" along with a minority of other non-Christian religions.

While it was not at all uncommon for US chaplains in the late eighteenth and early nineteenth centuries to be nondenominational, ordination credentials within a Christian denomination were eventually required, and today a formal denominational endorsement is necessary (or the equivalent from a religious association or fellowship of churches recognized by the Department of Defense). Christians, Jews, and Mormons have been commissioned as chaplains for some time now, and in 1994 the first Muslim was commissioned, in 2009 the first Buddhist, and in 2011 the first Hindu. Much has been made of the fact that declining numbers of Roman Catholic and mainline Protestant chaplains have produced a situation in which the number of evangelical chaplains is disproportionately large; and this representation has certainly shaped the way pluralism is constructed, contested, and defended

within the military, especially in relationship to the practice of
evangelism.

In the 1950s the National Association of Evangelicals (NAE)
endorsed the role of evangelicals in the military because it was "a
ripe harvest field" for evangelism. As Chaplain Barbara K. Sherer
observes in her study of fundamentalist chaplains in the military,
the NAE was also concerned that evangelicals not allow the pre-
dominance of Catholic chaplains to stand unchallenged. In the
words of the NAE at that time, "Evangelicals must not fail the
proportionately large number of men in the armed forces who are
anxious that the New Testament Gospel be preached, and a real
evangelistic work be carried on by our chaplains" (Sherer 2011, 7).

According to the Department of Defense, 33 percent of chaplains identify themselves as Southern Baptist, Pentecostal, or a
member of a denomination that is in the NAE while only 3 percent
of enlisted personnel and officers so identify (Townsend 2011a).
The Air Force reports, moreover, that 87 percent of those pursuing
chaplaincy attend evangelical divinity schools. Liberty University,
founded by Jerry Falwell Sr., has its own endorsing arm and now
trains one out of every five Air Force chaplain candidates studying
at an evangelical seminary (Townsend 2011b). The disproportionately high number of evangelical chaplains, therefore, is not
likely to change soon. Surveys consistently show that evangelicals
(including fundamentalists as a subset) typically exhibit strong
support for the United States and its military and do not communicate the kind of ambivalence or outright opposition to war found
among some members of mainline Protestant denominations. For
a number of reasons, evangelicals have less of a problem adopting
the motto of the Army Chaplains Corps, "*Pro Deo et Patria*" (For
God and Country). The problem, however, is that evangelicals and
fundamentalists also tend to be least comfortable with religious
pluralism. As the number of evangelical chaplains in the military
increases, the context once described by the NAE as a harvest field
has now become something more like a minefield.

Religious Rights and Freedoms

The pluralism characterizing the US military has been constructed and nurtured in the context of discourse about freedoms and rights. This is unsurprising, given the particular way that religion is positioned in relation to the state. As early as 1818, the constitutionality of the chaplaincy was challenged by Primitive Baptists under the Establishment Clause of the First Amendment ("Congress shall make no law respecting an establishment of religion, or preventing the free exercise thereof"). More recently, in 1985 two Harvard Law School students argued that the chaplaincy in effect put Congress in the position of establishing religion. The Second Circuit Court ruled that the Free Exercise Clause of the same amendment "obligates Congress, upon creating an Army, to make religion available to soldiers who have been moved to areas of the world where religion of their own denominations is not available to them" (Drazin and Currey 1995, 199). As conservative public policy scholar Hans Zeiger writes in defense of the chaplaincy, "Far from an establishment of religion, the chaplaincy is an essential bulwark of religious liberty" (2009).

The court went on to describe the chaplain's context as "a pluralistic military community." But precisely this pluralism poses significant challenges for chaplains who are required to minister to all service personnel while at the same time representing their own faith tradition. In 2010, at the order of Congress, the three branches of the military service merged their chaplain training schools into a single multifaith education center in Fort Jackson, South Carolina.[1] During training, chaplains receive four hours of instruction on the pluralistic context of the military and the constitutional basis for the chaplaincy, with another twenty hours

---

1. Susanne Schafer describes the center as having "'worship training labs' so instructors can discuss diverse faiths, with items brought from the various military schools. Golden icons line the walls in a small Greek Orthodox chapel; a Muslim prayer room is outfitted with prayer rugs and copies of the Quran; and a handwritten Jewish Torah is kept inside a wooden ark, alongside Sabbath candles and Seder plates to show how Passover is celebrated" (2010).

on topics that apply directly to ministry in a pluralistic context
(Sherer, 20).

While the "free exercise" rights of military personnel are ultimately the basis for legitimating the US military chaplaincy, other
justifications have been given, such as the role of chaplains in main-
taining and supporting troop morale, providing daily counseling,
fulfilling the ever-evolving and expanding roles in other aspects
of military operations and advising, and functioning as a "social
conscience" within the military—though the latter is necessarily
muted by the very nature of the fact that all chaplains are commissioned as officers. According to Kim Hansen, who has produced
a remarkable study of the US military chaplaincy:

> As officers, chaplains are not supposed to comment on national
> policy. It is axiomatic that a secure democracy must have armed
> forces subservient to civilian leadership which makes it wrong for
> the commissioned military hierarchy to dissent. If chaplains seem
> to assent to unholy actions, it's not necessarily because they are
> dependent on the military for their livelihood or compromising
> to protect their careers. More likely, it is because they understand
> that the prophetic voice, whether grounded in civil religion or
> religion proper, is muted by the necessary depoliticization of the
> professional officer corps. (2012, 31)

It is also true, as Hansen notes, that self-selection yields a chaplain corps that is "safe to have around" (31). Clergy with pacifist
leanings or who find it more difficult to serve God and country
simultaneously tend not to volunteer. The history of the chaplaincy
includes a long line of chaplains who have been able to employ
religious faith as a means of blessing and validating the military
operations of the nation or empire it serves (cf. Bergen 2004). At
the same time, the majority of interviews with chaplains that I
have read or conducted reveal that most understand their calling
primarily as a service to enlisted personnel rather than to the nation. They spend most of their time providing spiritual guidance,

religious services, and counseling. Yet in precisely these ways chaplains play a critical role in advancing troops' military readiness not only by boosting morale and mental health but also through the peaceful integration of military and spiritual values. As Hansen puts it, "Dressed in officers' uniforms, chaplains advance a civil religion that is inclusive and inoffensive, preaching a spirituality that is bland and generic compared to the particular faith groups they represent and draw on in the worship services they provide" (34).

One unique and evolving feature of US military chaplaincy, related to religious pluralism, is the way chaplains are increasingly called on to play the role of cross-cultural and interreligious mediators and liaisons, thereby placing a greater demand on their capacity for tolerating religious diversity. Chaplains are at times asked to work with diverse faith communities in foreign countries, to advise their commanders in areas where they can be useful tactically—for example, in reducing interreligious tensions that complicate military missions—and to improve and inform perceptions of persons outside the United States. To be sure, chaplains are often limited in what they are allowed to do, and some commanding officers resist expanding an "operational" role for chaplains. Yet, according to Undersecretary of Defense for Personnel and Readiness, Dr. David Chu, "Whereas in the past, chaplains would probably be called upon to function as practitioners in their individual faith traditions; in the future, they will increasingly be called upon to be consultants and advisors . . . to their commanders on the precepts of other world religions." According to Chu, endorsing denominations must therefore embrace a certain degree of pluralism: "Their conceptual picture of ministry must clearly depict a very pluralistic mindset reflecting pluralism in their own ranks and in the world in which we function" (cited in Zeiger).

Civil Religion

Military chaplains also have an important civic role. Chaplains participate in a variety of military ceremonies (commissionings, dedications, graduations, memorials, public holiday observances, and so on). But while these are generally not understood to be religious in a formal sense, "nowhere is civil religion both created and celebrated more than in the Armed Forces; nothing is more hallowed to Americans or to war veterans than what Lincoln called 'these honored dead.' The Chaplain is a guardian not only of his particular faith, but of the common American faith—in democracy, liberty, and justice" (Zeiger).

The mention here of civil religion is important, even though it does not frequently enter the picture in textbook discussions of religious pluralism. If civil religion really is a religion, however, it is probably the most influential and powerful of them because it is pervasive. Especially within the US military, in the context of a manifest plurality, civil religion provides a unity of symbols, beliefs, and rituals. Carolyn Marvin and David Ingle call nationalism "the most powerful religion in the US and, perhaps in many other countries." Nationalism, they claim, "satisfies many traditional definitions of religion, but citizens of nation-states have religious reasons for denying it" (1996, 767). They go on to ask,

> If nationalism is religious, why do we deny it? Because what is obligatory for group members must be separated, as holy things are, from what is contestable. To concede that nationalism is a religion is to expose it to challenge, to make it just the same as sectarian religion. By explicitly denying that our national symbols and duties are sacred, we shield them from competition with sectarian symbols. In so doing, we embrace the ancient command not to speak the sacred, ineffable name of god. That god is inexpressible, unsayable, unknowable, beyond language. But that god may not be refused when it calls for sacrifice. (770)

On one level, civil religion, or the religion of "nationalism," is ubiquitous and dominant in US culture; yet on another level, it is utterly invisible and unrecognizable for what it is. It borrows from Christian symbols and practices but recasts them in a nondescript way so that the god venerated and the spirituality fostered is less particular (though no less demanding). This renders it remarkably powerful, flexible, and resilient in shaping values, directing energy, and providing a broader (and shared) framework for constructing pluralism. As the religious landscape within the United States has changed over the last two hundred years, so has the role various religions play in the nation's public life. William Hutchison describes this change as a movement from mere "toleration," at the beginning of the nation's history, toward "inclusion" and now, in the last half century, toward a new "pluralism of participation" (2003, 6). By rallying around the nation as the unquestioned point of unity, subordinate only to a generic god who guides and blesses the nation and in whom the collective "we" of the nation trusts, civil religion provides the rituals, symbols, and moral coordinates (preserving rights and freedoms, patriotism, and so on) for enacting this new "pluralism of participation."

Politicians and celebrities often play important roles in superintending how civil religion is the arbiter of pluralism in the United States.[2] Yet Zeiger is certainly correct that military chaplains play a critical role as guardians not only of their own particular faith traditions "but of the common American faith." Indeed, it is the heartbeat of civil religion to render these two "faiths" compatible (if not identical) so that civic virtue is the same as religious virtue. As Hansen points out, "What military chaplains do is throw martial virtues into the mix, so that military virtues [for example, "honor," "courage," or "commitment"] also look like good citizenship and good Christianity" (28). As one Southern

2. Take for instance "A Prayer for America," the national interfaith service of mourning held in Yankee Stadium on September 23, 2001, twelve days after the attacks on the World Trade Center. The event included invocations, blowing the Jewish shofar (ram's horn), prayers, readings, reflections, and benedictions from Protestant, Catholic, Greek Orthodox, Jewish, Muslim, Hindu, and Sikh faiths interspersed with patriotic and inspirational songs, along with solemn and defiant remarks from Mayor Giuliani, Governor George Pataki, and Admiral Robert Natter. Note, however, how the event was hosted from beginning to end by Oprah Winfrey, who served much like the high priestess of American civil religion.

Baptist chaplain puts it: "There are things worth dying for. OK? Many, even in our House and Senate today, would say there maybe aren't things worth dying for. Because liberalism ultimately leads to that road. . . . If there's anybody who needs to think there's things worth dying for it is marines who will be asked to do that one day" (Hansen, 29).

The challenge, of course, is the notoriously thin line between the position that serving God and serving country are compatible and the practice of treating them as one and the same. Indeed, the very nature of civil religion blurs the distinction. When the nation becomes an absolute value for which Christians will die and kill (and frequently kill other Christians), then we are surely justified in asking whether that line has been crossed.

Evangelism in the US Military

The pluralism enacted within the US military, then, is narrated by the discourse of modern liberal rights and freedoms coupled with a default civil religion that tolerates religious diversity but positions and domesticates that diversity toward promoting the nation-state. Within this complex pluralistic context, recent battles over evangelizing in the military have arisen. For if it is true that the chaplaincy exists within a pluralistic military community to ensure that all soldiers are able to practice the free exercise of religion, it is also true that chaplains who do not embrace this pluralism, or who at least cannot tolerate it and cooperate within it, pose a threat to the constitutional ground on which the chaplaincy stands (Drazin and Currey, 10–11).

Evangelism or Proselytism?

One way chaplains have dealt with this problem is by trying to maintain an almost impossible distinction between "evangelism" and "proselytism." "Evangelism," in this way of parsing things, refers to efforts to convert those who are not affiliated with a religious body, which is permissible, while "proselytism" refers to efforts to convert those who are affiliated, which is not permissible. A code of ethics is followed in these matters, which was written by a private association of religious bodies that provides chaplains to the military. (This code is called the National Conference on Ministry to the Armed Forces, or NCMAF.) Until recently, this code contained the following statement: "I will not proselytize from other religious bodies, but I retain the right to evangelize those who are not affiliated" (Cooperman 2005, A3). Naturally, there is plenty of gray area here since some atheists and freethinkers have their own associations and do not necessarily consider themselves unaffiliated, nor do they tend to welcome evangelism directed their way even if they were unaffiliated. The Defense Department never officially sponsored the code, but it was regularly handed out at chaplains' schools until 2005 when the Air Force was sued over a growing number of charges about anti-Semitism, preferential treatment for Christians (and evangelicals in particular), the promotion of prayer, and high pressure among cadets to convert to evangelical Christianity by senior cadets, faculty, and staff.

Though the current version of the NCMAF covenant no longer retains the word "proselytize," it is clear from studies on chaplaincy and interviews with chaplains that the principle is still widely accepted. As Hansen observes, however, "The difficulty with the self-imposed prohibition against proselytization isn't so much whether there should be one but the fact that chaplains don't agree on what *proselytization* means" (60). This produces situations in which some chaplains are seen by others as overstepping the line, but they justify themselves because they do not see themselves as proselytizing but as evangelizing or, to use another favorite word, "witnessing." Add to this the views held by some evangelicals that certain Christian groups are not really Christians in the first place, and one can readily see the complexity of evangelism within the pluralistic context of the military.

Chaplains and Diverse Roles

To be sure, many if not most chaplains spend much of their time counseling and report that the typical concerns voiced in those counseling sessions are not necessarily religious. Many chaplains, therefore, are likely not to see the practice of evangelism (or proselytization) as foregrounded in their work, if they see it as present at all. As one Catholic chaplain puts it, "I'm not out to make a whole bunch of Catholics. I'm not out to make a whole bunch of anything, except to help them be the best men and women they can be. And to do the best job that they can do. To be the best husbands, to be the best wives, i.e., to make America a much better place. That's my approach" (Hansen, 60). And yet it is precisely the nature of the chaplaincy to bring religious or spiritual perspectives to any given situation, and the answer to the question of when exactly a chaplain is "evangelizing" in those contexts is complex if not incorrigibly fuzzy.

The role of the military chaplain, who both represents the church and is commissioned and paid by the state, is an extraordinary and complex case study when considered in terms of an ethics of evangelism. Countless chaplains are effective witnesses to Christ as they strive to advocate for the needs of those they serve and to provide spiritual care and liturgical and ritual services. Many chaplains struggle to help soldiers find some moral purpose in their duties (though some find that remarkably easier to do than others). Many chaplains take great care to avoid securing conversions from among those under their care who are especially vulnerable, and instead many speak of evangelism in terms of a "ministry of presence" (Totten 2013, 19) by which they gain the rapport and trust of the enlisted. As Andrew Todd puts it, speaking in the context of the British military, "Faith is communicated by being as much as by doing; and by example, rather than by seeking to convert" (2013, 10).

At the same time, there is no way to avoid the fact that chaplains are not only members of a nation's military and bearers of its uniforms; they advance the mission of that nation and its military. If their incarnational presence is carried out well, "through their pastoral, ritual, and moral presence, chaplains become 'force multipliers'—they contribute, whether intentionally or not, to the military effectiveness of the unit" (Todd, 5).

Within the long history of military chaplaincy, some chaplains have embraced the role of enhancing military effectiveness with great passion. Mark Hayden, in his fascinating study of German military chaplains in World War II, notes that while some chaplains considered their priestly function to be primary (for example, one of the tasks assigned to chaplains was to be present with those soldiers condemned to be executed for whatever reason), chaplains were at the same time expected to build morale, preach patriotic sermons, and provide legitimacy to the regime, a regime that laid claim to divine mandate, as illustrated in the slogan "God is with us" engraved on every military belt buckle (2005, 43–44). Yet we know from reports of captured chaplains that even with heavy layers of propaganda (religious and otherwise) justifying the Nazi cause, some believed the war to be criminal but carried on their work of chaplaincy out of hope for the personnel they served.

Chaplaincy as Litigious

The present context of religious pluralism in the US military makes the evangelistic ministry of the chaplain even more complicated than in previous historical contexts. Insofar as religious pluralism is narrated by the discourse of rights in the context of the military, we find that, on one hand, atheists and non-Christians sue the military because they claim to be discriminated against, forced to participate in public prayers, blocked for promotions, and violated with respect to religious freedoms. Evangelicals, on the other hand, sue the military because they claim their First Amendment rights to evangelize and to invoke the name of Jesus in public prayer are curtailed.

For these and other reasons, it should be no surprise that the chaplaincy has become an increasingly litigious environment with some evangelical chaplains challenging the promotion of pluralism within the military, saying it restricts their "fundamental right, constitutionally protected by the First Amendment, to evangelize or proselytize both in the military and among foreign populations" (Whitt 2012, 53). In other words, not only does a particular discourse of freedoms and rights narrate the kind of religious pluralism we find within the US military, it also comes to narrate how evangelism is practiced within that context. Chaplains' ministry is performed at the intersection of the Constitution's Establishment Clause, on one hand, and its Free Exercise Clause, on the other. The peaceful, corporate, and embodied offer of Christ that empties itself of power and privilege is thus transformed into a competitive practice in which the evangelist not only demands a right to evangelize but also calls on the state to secure that right. The dialectic dramatically reveals just how habituated to state-sponsored pluralism the practice of evangelism can and has become.

Public Prayer

Most controversies that arise in relation to religious pluralism in the military pertain either to the practice of evangelism or to some chaplains' insistence on praying in the name of Jesus not only in worship services but also in official ceremonies, which necessarily include non-Christians. In 2006, Captain Jonathan Stertzbach, an evangelical field artillery chaplain, gave an interview to the *Washington Times* in which he discussed his being asked by a brigade chaplain to pray at a memorial service for a fallen soldier but to "modify" his prayers to begin with, "Please pray according to your faith as I pray according to mine," and to end with "in Thy name we pray." He was allowed to add, "and in Jesus's name I pray" (Duin 2006). It is striking how Christians in a range of public settings—and now even in their own churches—have begun to use the odd phrase "in thy [or your] name we pray," a self-contradictory benediction that purports to pray in a "name" but then doesn't use the name! Christians have clearly not yet figured out just how we are to pray in pluralistic contexts. Stertzbach was removed from his preaching responsibilities at the chapel for speaking to the *Washington Times* about the incident. Without commenting directly on the case, Martha Rudd, spokesperson for the Army, said, "There are some people who are uncomfortable with pluralism. . . . And if a chaplain is uncomfortable with that, he or she should find a ministry outside of the military" (Pulliam 2006). In 2010, the House entertained (though ultimately rejected) an amendment to the Military Construction Authorization Act proposed by Representative Michele Bachmann to allow military chaplains to close their prayers "according to the dictates of the chaplain's own conscience" in an effort to lend support to those Christians who wish to pray "in Jesus's name" at public, nonreligious military events. Other cases could be mentioned in this connection, such as that of Navy chaplain Lt. Gordon Klingenschmitt, who has made a cottage industry out of his being discharged for "daring" to use the name of Jesus in public prayers (he was court-martialed in 2006 for "disobeying an order" when attending a rally in front of the White House dressed in Navy uniform).

Chaplains who insist on leading public prayers in pluralistic contexts by explicitly claiming "in Jesus's name we pray" may believe that they are exercising a faithful witness to Christ. Some even thrive on the offense such language gives as sure proof of their fidelity to Christ. In the context of pluralism as negotiated in the United States, however, it is worth asking how the mere mention of Jesus's name has come to carry so much of the freight of Christian witness (especially among evangelicals).[3] Something has

---

3. The recent "Finding Faith Today" survey shows that only 35 percent of evangelicals focus their description of what it means to be a Christian on a way of living and acting as compared with 55 percent of Roman Catholics and 65 percent of mainline Protestants. Evangelicals are far more likely to associate what it means to be a Christian with adopting a particular set of beliefs, having a personal relationship

gone wrong when Christians offer little resistance when asked by a nation or empire to kill on its behalf while their right to utter Jesus's name in public must be protected at all costs. Chaplains who assert their rights to evangelize or pray publicly in Jesus's name may be venerated as hero-saints and put on the speaking circuit in churches and conventions. But as William Cavanaugh observes, "Religious and lethal devotion to the unity of the nation-state itself is assumed to be a normal part of one's civic duties" (2011, 55).

The Freedoms and Rights of Pluralism

What we see in the US context, and especially in the military as an intense microcosm, is a pluralism constructed on the premise of freedoms and rights possessed by individuals *as* individuals and guaranteed by the state, which positions those individuals in direct relation to itself. But the discourse of rights is problematic, at least when framing the practice of evangelism. While the Bible never uses the language of rights, there is a Christian tradition of rights, as Daniel Bell has shown, which was first articulated in Aquinas and embodied in medieval monastic communities, such as the Cistercians (Bell 2001, 103). For Aquinas, however, a divine ordering of the human community in terms of a "common good" precedes the notion of individual rights. As Bell puts it, "Right was fundamentally a matter of consent to or participation in the divine order and the individual was understood as possessed by Christ and a recipient of all the good that one is, has, and does" (105). But this is a very different tradition and discourse than the more individualistic versions developed by modern social contract theorists that are the legacy of the Enlightenment and of modernity. For the latter, Bell says that "society was rightly understood as constituted by a conglomeration of rights and duties adhering to the individual over against the whole. . . . According to

---

with Jesus, or accepting Jesus into one's heart. See slide 8 at http://www.bu.edu/sth/files/2017/08/2017-08-20-Finding-Faith-Today.pdf.

this conception, the individual occupies the central position as right is associated with a human power to control and dispose of temporal things. Individuals, in other words, become essentially proprietors" (105).

For this reason, in the case of modern liberal rights, "human social relations were increasingly acquisitive, atomistic, and competitive" (105), and so the common good was reduced to an increasingly thin, or even empty, coordination of individual rights over against one another and over against the larger social whole.

Rights Grounded in the Common Good

Perhaps in pluralistic contexts such as modern democracies, this thin coordination of individual rights is as much of a "shared" vision as we can hope for. It must be said that the characteristically modern assertion and protection of individual rights (expressed, for example, in terms of free speech, free exercise of religion, etc.) as somehow "inalienable" has achieved great good in the world, including liberatory movements and work for justice embedded in civil rights efforts. But Christians who have led movements for the rights of women, ethnic and racial minority groups, farm workers, or LGBTQ persons have typically drawn deeply on more substantive visions of a common good, visions that precede and ground any talk of individual rights. That common good might, for example, be articulated in terms of the shalom announced by the Hebrew prophets, the coming of God's reign announced by Jesus, or even a symbol as potent as Martin Luther King Jr.'s Beloved Community. This theological grounding does not mean that Christians do not or cannot make common cause with people who seek rights on the basis of "natural rights," attaching to individuals as such. But rights-seeking Christians draw on a more substantive and communal grounding of individual rights from within and authorized by a divinely established common good.

The "right" to evangelize (as remarkable as that should sound to us) unfortunately participates in the more atomistic and competitive tradition that attempts to secure a place for itself in the world. In important ways this positioning of evangelism by state-sponsored individual rights and freedoms eclipses the church as a mediating institution and as a transnational body from which Christians might instead draw their primary identities. This eclipse has powerful implications for evangelism, as ecclesial identity is subordinated to a higher citizenship and set of national allegiances rendered sacred and ultimate by the rituals of American civil religion. As the body of Christ ceases to provide the primary political imagination and source of unity for Christians, private markers of Christian identity become more important, while evangelism is practiced as the offer of a fundamentally individualistic and largely interior salvation with little intrinsic connection to ecclesial life or identity. The church is relegated to a secondary and instrumental relationship to salvation, and evangelism is inevitably shorn of its prophetic character as it is rendered compatible with the nation's claims on us and its demand for our obedience and sacrifice.

Meanwhile the state offers its own political imagination, its own unity, and its own common good, which is little more than the relatively thin coordination of individual rights and freedoms. But without a substantive common good, as Cavanaugh observes, "plurality is not simply a promise but a threat, one that must be met by an even greater pull toward unity." What is the source of that unity? "It can only be that the nation-state becomes an end in itself, a kind of transcendent reference needed to bind the many to each other" (2011, 47). The state then becomes a kind of savior:

> In the absence of shared ends, devotion to the nation-state as the end in itself becomes ever more urgent. The nation-state *needs* the constant crisis of pluralism in order to enact the *unum* [one]. Indeed, the constant threat of disorder is crucial to any state that defines its indispensability in terms of the security it offers. Pluralism will always be a crisis for the liberal state, and the solution to the crisis of pluralism is to rally around the nation-state, the locus of mystical communion that rescues us from the conflicts of civil society. (53)

The Church and the Pluralistic Imagination

Christians have no reason to fear or oppose religious diversity and plurality for the sake of evangelism. Yet Christians cannot allow themselves to become habituated to a pluralistic imagination that presupposes the false unity imposed by the nation and the civil religion it sponsors. The good news does not need the help of the state just as it does not need the privileges of empire. Such help and privilege too often come with the strings of violence and competition attached.

Christians treasure the hospitality of others so that the good news can be shared freely in our world. We also seek to provide that hospitality to others, and we actively seek to nurture societies where persons of all faiths can openly and nonviolently share their faith and hope with others. But Christians seek no privileged position for themselves in the world, no cultural leverage that would compel or coerce others to receive or accept our good news. At the same time, Christians cannot accept a pluralism that positions the church or its good news under the larger canopy of civil religion. Instead, we seek to live within the pluralistic imagination of a church catholic—one in which we attempt to live peaceably with our neighbors, including neighbors of other faiths. We bear visible, nonviolent, and embodied witness to Christ throughout the world just as we seek patiently to receive the witness of others. But evangelistic patience and openness does not mean we must allow the church to be positioned by the counterfeit unities of empire, nation, or market.

6

Evangelism and Nonviolence

In the June 14, 2003, issue of the *Christian Century*, editor John M. Buchanan replied to letters his magazine had been receiving, which objected to advertisements placed in the magazine for military chaplaincy.[1] Said Buchanan, "Some have argued that military chaplaincy is objectionable on moral grounds and probably unconstitutional. Others have been distressed by the way the chaplain in the ads seems to be blessing military activity. Some accused us of caving in to the culture of war and concluded that we'd probably advertise anything so long as the customer paid the price" (3). Buchanan cited his own ambivalence on the question of military chaplaincy as well as conversations he had held with chaplains. He concluded, "Christians are involved in this world. Being a faithful Christian means risking getting one's hands dirty. I've learned to respect those who minister to people in the military, even if I may disagree with what the military is doing. The actions of the military, and the role of chaplains, are issues we will continue to

1. My thanks to Andrew Burd-Harris, whose master's thesis alerted me to this editorial.

address in the content of the magazine. And we'll continue to run ads for military chaplaincy."

Responses to Buchanan in the following July 26 issue were mostly supportive. One chaplain's response described the chaplaincy as "a mission field. . . . An opportunity to be 'priestly' and to be 'prophetic.'" The chaplain went on to say,

> Each day in the life of an officer and an enlisted man or woman there is an opportunity to influence a decision, address an ethical issue and to offer comfort and hope. We are able to earn the trust of our servicemen and women because we live with them, work with them and share their hardships. I dread to think what life would be like without the presence of clergy in uniform. Each day, there are chaplains who reluctantly don the Nathan role and confront the Davids—the leadership—with the prophetic word. Those who stand outside the armed services—and even those who serve in them—may never know that is happening, but it happens. (James P. Nickols)

Another letter to the editor described military chaplains as "bright, thoughtful people with a commitment to peace. They know the price that war extracts from all sides of a battle and seek to avoid conflict if possible." He continues,

> I have made public my opposition to the war in Iraq, but I do not believe that doing so precludes support for troops called on to fight it and their families. We need military chaplains to help our troops clarify and maintain values of compassion and to return with as little psychological damage from the trauma of warfare as possible, to become productive members of society. (Duane H. Fickeisen)

And yet another reader wrote,

> Like many of your readers, I was disturbed by the advertisements for military chaplaincy. How can a man or woman who has taken a vow to proclaim the gospel of Jesus Christ work for the military?

The answer was pointed out to me by a teenager in my congregation who asked, "Don't you have a responsibility to be a pastor to people you don't agree with? Isn't that what you tell us—that we are called to care for all people no matter who they are?" (Robert W. Lowry)

As illustrated by these responses, the original editorial, and the original opposition to the ads to which the editorial responded, military chaplaincy is a complex issue for Christians. The military chaplain's situation is undoubtedly unique, and most Christians will never face the complex challenges that chaplains face in negotiating pluralism as they bear witness to Christ in their particular context. Likewise, the chaplain's relationship to violence is unique and unlike what most other Christians experience as a context for their witness: providing liturgical services for troops, offering counsel for those who struggle with the demands of military service, memorializing the fallen, and responding in healing ways to those dealing with the trauma of war and other military operations.

At the same time, chaplaincy is not simply a role unique to the military context but is instead a posture with which Christians and their churches have become comfortable for the better part of two millennia. Sustaining that posture for any length of time (to say nothing of two millennia) requires what might be called an "ethics of chaplaincy" for which the radical claims of Christ on our lives are subordinated to or rendered compatible with the mission of the nation or empire in which we find ourselves. This includes, most critically, a rationalization of and willingness to use violence in the service of that nation or empire.

These deeper questions of ultimate allegiance and violence are decisive for all Christians, not just military chaplains, especially for those of us who live in contexts where Christendom arrangements still have a strong footing. They are questions about the integrity of Christian witness and whether (or to what extent) that witness is compromised by the adoption of violence as a way of living life, resolving conflict, and achieving peace. Buchanan may well be right that "being a faithful Christian means risking getting one's hands dirty." The question, however, is whether we are called to get our hands bloody.

The "Peace" of Empires

While empires enact their so-called "peace" through violence, their militaries cannot be made a scapegoat, nor do I have any interest in dishonoring those who serve or have served in the military. The modern US military is far more complex than such a scapegoating would allow, involved as it is in all sorts of civil, humanitarian, and relief work both in the United States and abroad. But even beyond that complexity, the military, in carrying out the ambitions of empire, must also be viewed as something more like a consequence or a symptom than as the cause of a culture's commitment to violence.

I have immense respect for military chaplains who attempt to practice evangelism in their context. However, my studies of and conversations with chaplains lead me to be wary of how a posture of chaplaincy tends to deform evangelistic practice by eclipsing the necessarily prophetic dimensions of that witness where ultimate allegiances are concerned. Again, though, a posture of chaplaincy has characterized much of Christian witness for centuries, and there is no good reason for focusing the blame on either the military or its particular forms of chaplaincy.

Christian Formation and Violence

If we are to ask about the shape of the Christian's faithfulness in a culture disposed to the use of violence, we must instead look closely at the deeper loyalty and violence asked of us all in exchange for the peace of empire or nation. If ours can be described as an age of individualism, it is ironically also an age that is deeply tribalistic, and as jingoistic as it ever was where nationality is concerned. This is especially true in the post–9/11 United States, where the attacks on US soil had an enormous effect in shoring up the nation as the altar of American civil religion on which its citizens are asked to make sacrifices that are nothing less than acts of worship.

This trust in the nation and a corresponding disposition toward violence require a comprehensive formation advanced by the military, to be sure. But it is already present and perpetuated in our culture through our families, schools, movies and entertainment, and, of course, our religious institutions. Both civilians and soldiers must be trained to believe in violence as useful and redemptive. While the military plays a critical role in providing that formation, our society provides the prior and comprehensive formation into patriots—loyal servants of the nation and believers in its holiness and goodness. For persons of faith, this means believing that God, the military, and the nation are inextricably linked and mutually supportive. The military cannot be wholly blamed for this formation, nor are military personnel those who have somehow been uniquely or grotesquely deformed in the ways of violence. In the context of nationalism, the comprehensive formation toward violence is shared by all.

The church, however, has not always shared this bent. At several points in Christian history, the question of the Christian's relationship to the military has been posed in regard to the church's evangelistic witness. This question was posed as Christians asked whether they should serve in the military, and many concluded they could not. This was an urgent question for the first Christians, and their refusal to serve was a central and distinctive part of their identity, often contributing to their persecution. That question hardly even comes up for US Christians today, however, so accustomed are we to our posture as chaplains of the empire and so confident are we in the goods it can deliver to us and others around the globe. As with other Christians throughout history, we believe that our empire is somehow different from others, perhaps even God ordained, and the grand exception. This exceptionalism

then allows us to support not only defensive action but even pre-
emptive and policing violence around the globe.

But a second and perhaps more illuminating way of framing the
question of the Christian's relationship to the military is not to ask
whether Christians should serve in the military but to ask why any
decent military in the world would have us.[2] This, in fact, is another
important way the question has been posed: from the standpoint
of the empire or nation rather than from the standpoint of the
Christians. There are many good reasons to ask the question in
this way. After all, one of the distinguishing characteristics, if not
the distinguishing characteristic, of those who follow the teachings and example of Jesus Christ is their resolve not to kill their
enemies. The messiah whom Christians follow and into whose life
we seek to be formed commanded us to turn the other cheek and
to put away the sword when tempted to use it. He commanded
us instead to love, pray for, and forgive our enemies, something
many of us find difficult to do while simultaneously killing them.
Killing one's enemies also makes evangelizing them a bit tricky.

For the most part, Christians have believed that government is a
legitimate and God-ordained feature of human existence to which
we are called to be subject. But at several crucial points, especially
when it comes to doing violence to others, Christians have found
ourselves needing to obey God rather than humans and finding it
impossible, as Jesus said, "to serve two masters." In the context
of empire, as noted earlier, this led to the confession that Jesus is
Lord and the emperor is not. But can Christians really be trusted
then? What serious military in the world would have a group of
persons whose hallmark is love of their enemies?

In earlier chapters, I discussed the relationship of empire to
evangelism and suggested ways that empire deforms evangelistic

2. Stanley Hauerwas, in "Why Gays (as a Group) Are Morally Superior to Christians (as a Group)," argues, somewhat tongue-in-cheek, that when it comes to military
service, he as a pacifist finds it "a wonderful thing that some people are excluded as
a group." Says Hauerwas, "I only wish that Christians could be seen by the military
to be as problematic as gays" (2001, 519).

practice through its totalizing and colonizing project throughout the world, a project in which Christianity has often served
as chaplain. I suggested that this project is carried out not only
through military conquest but through mechanisms of control
and influence that are economic, cultural, psychological, and even
religious. But even if empire extends its influence throughout the
world by these means, rather than by war and conquest, there is
certainly no more prominent instance of the empire substituting
itself as Lord than when it asks Christians to kill for it or to do
violence to others on its behalf (and frequently, as history shows,
against fellow Christians). At this point the empire has made itself
into an absolute value (cf. Carter 2001, 157).

Nations function similarly, so that we find ourselves ritually
singing songs of loyalty and pledging our undying allegiance,
speaking reverently with words like heart and soul, sacrifice, and
providence. We adorn our clothes, buildings, and possessions with
its symbols, and, as difficult as it is to believe, our church sanc-
tuaries. I have even attended a church service in Texas where the
American flag was processed into the sanctuary behind the cross
on Flag Day. I have also attended a worship service in Oklahoma
where, because it was the Fourth of July, instead of an opening
prayer or invocation, the pastor led the congregation in the pledge
of allegiance to the flag. One would like to think that Christians
in the context of modern empire struggle with questions of dual
citizenship, but there is not always much struggle going on.

The commonwealth of God has been imaginatively fused with
the nation-state for so long that we are nearly unable to see that
killing because the nation has asked us to renders an act of worship
that is just as real, if not more so, than when the first Christians
were asked to burn a pinch of incense to the emperor. We need not
go all the way back to the fourth century to find a precedent for our
willingness to make the empire or the nation-state an absolute value.

Many consider Germany under the leadership of Hitler to be
the surest way to refute the position of Christian pacifists. Surely

here is a case where killing was morally required by Christians. But this line of reasoning fails to account for how a disposition toward violence and nation-idolatry among Christians was capable of inventing, or at least sustaining, someone like Hitler in the first place. After all, it was not Hitler himself who carried out mass killings or invaded nations but Christians who marched on his orders. And we should recall that Germany was one of the most devoutly Christian nations in the world at the time.

Plenty of evidence shows that Hitler and many of his senior officers had nothing but contempt for Christianity; but what cannot be disputed is the fact that his plans could never have been carried out without the mobilization of hundreds of thousands of Christians, for whom allegiance to God had been fused with allegiance to the nation—complete with songs, oaths, and lots and lots of flags. This also includes approximately one thousand Protestant and Catholic clergy who served as chaplains in the German military during World War II (Bergen 2001, 233). Time and time again, Christians in the modern era have demonstrated that the nation-state is for us, as Cavanaugh has suggested, "a fetish." We will die for it. And we will kill for it (1998, 195–96).

A Pacifist Ethics versus an Ethics of Chaplaincy

An ethics of chaplaincy has the potential to undercut and ultimately derail the practice of evangelism both by substituting Christ's claim on our lives with that of some other sovereign entity and by accepting as a given the Christian's (and indeed the church's) formation by a pervasive culture of violence, war-making, and coercion. In contrast to an ethics of chaplaincy, the ethics of evangelism I advocate is intrinsically pacifist. While at first it may sound strange to use that word in the context of evangelism, it is important to understand pacifism as a form of public witness to the good news that is logically prior to any consideration of whether to use violence. For the Christian, peace is not only the content of our evangelism; it is its very form. Jesus directly condemns or refuses violence in the Gospel stories, but what he rejects is not just violence but the raising to ultimacy of legitimate purposes that leads us to rationalize harming others in attaining those purposes. Here we encounter one of the most important features of a pacifist ethics: it is an ethics of means. Peace, in other words, is not for the Christian simply an *end* we seek such that we are then free to employ whatever *means* we might calculate will effectively secure that end. Rather, in Christ, we have been given a peaceful *way* (and so the first Christians could refer to Christianity as "the way"). Pacifism here is not a sentimental posture that naively believes in the utility of nonviolence for achieving peace in the world, though there are many compelling examples of the effectiveness of pacifism in history. There is no guarantee, and we have been given no promise, that a commitment to Christ's way of nonviolence will make the world a less violent place. On the contrary, the pacifism practiced by Christians is not an ethic that is adopted because we calculate that it will "work" but a subordination of the entire calculus of effectiveness to Christ's way.

The relationship between means and end, or cause and effect, turns out to be critically important for an ethics of evangelism and indeed for all Christian ethics, especially when considered in relation to violence. For the Christian is called to live from a distinctive vision of cause and effect narrated by the story of Jesus's life rather than what is most effective in relation to a particular end that we might posit. As Yoder once said, "The relationship between the obedience of God's people and the triumph of God's cause is not a relationship of cause and effect but one of cross and resurrection" (1972, 238). For that reason, the truth of Christianity cannot be secured or validated by appeals to its credibility or usefulness as measured by supposedly wider or foundational criteria in experience and reason. Of course, we would all like to think that the way of Christ is helpful and intelligent. The temptation is strong to want people not only to understand us but "to have to believe us" (287). After all, if the good news about Christ is true, surely it must be widely plausible, if not downright irresistible. Yet in accepting that sort of logic, we end up, over time, accommodating the radical way of Christ to a set of vague moral principles or a baseline code of conduct that an unbelieving world can accept without being transformed by Christ and empowered by God's Spirit.

Within the ethics of chaplaincy made possible by an imperial social imagination, the church comes to see itself as responsible to and for the larger society. But this happens in such a way that the Christian ethic is premised on answering, What sort of ethic can be asked of everyone, regardless of whether they follow Christ? Christological pacifism, by contrast, while it is "for everyone" in the sense of being available to everyone and offered as the way of Christ for everyone, requires a lived confession of Christ's messiahship and a participation in the new social reality that is Christ's body. Within an imperial social imagination, however, the embarrassingly particular nature of the Christian's confession and loyalty is subordinated to a more universal and transcendent set of values that better suit the logic of empire and underwrite its totalizing project.

A pacifist ethics of evangelism does not fear but rather embraces the vulnerability we see in the cross as intrinsic to its offer. What Christians have to offer the world can only be offered nonviolently. Pacifist Christians will not do "whatever it takes" to ensure the reception of their witness. To accomplish God's purposes, in other words, God does not need our violence, but instead desires our worship and our faithfulness. By contrast, our loyalty to nation and our attachment to the economic wealth and liberties secured by it are frequently idolatrous and therefore false objects of worship that require our violence for their protection. Approaches to evangelism that try to eliminate the gospel's refusability by diminishing the scandal of a God who saves through love and humility may appear to be more universal and inviting. But it is not clear that reducing the gospel to what people already believe and how they already act is really a faithful offer of good news.

Evangelism, then, is intrinsically related to a pacifist ethics precisely because evangelism requires that we exemplify God's peace if we are to faithfully and credibly offer God's peace to the world. This is all the truer since the whole of our lives and not just some parts are to be governed by the peace of Christ. For all that a Christian is and does is a witness to the gospel and may thus be properly taken as evangelistic. The ethics of evangelism and a broader pacifist ethics are also related in regard to empires or nation-states that extend and maintain themselves through war, acts of violence, and imperial stories justifying violence as necessary, inescapable, and even redemptive. Christians do not seek to be subversive or nonconformist; but insofar as the Christian's witness is fundamentally one of peace, an inescapable contradiction exists between the practice of evangelism and the violence of empire.

To argue for a pacifist ethics of evangelism is to claim that a Christian ethics is an ethics of witness rather than an ethics of results; it is an acquired habit of counting for naught all we once figured for gain. It is an embodied conviction that in the life, death, and resurrection of Jesus we have discovered a God who saves the world through patience and peace. A Christian ethics is also an ethics premised on a hope that is fixed on the resurrection of Christ. Only this unseen hope can give meaning and purpose to our nonviolence. This hope does not mean that our lives are oriented toward some blind, futuristic, utopian dream that enables us passively to accept present injustice. But that hope provides a challenge to our assumptions that violence is unavoidable, and it also challenges our inability or refusal to imagine alternatives to violence. A resurrection hope points to a transcendent horizon that is never to be equated with our own solutions or reduced to strategies based on short-term calculations of efficacy. This resurrection hope enables us to courageously envision and enact imaginative responses to violence that otherwise would be impossible because they are inconceivable. By forgoing the coercive means that present themselves to us as potentially able to secure the truth of our convictions, a resurrection hope instead requires us to rely on God's promises rather than enact our frantic need to secure results. In doing so, we bear witness to a more real world in which Christ is risen and violence is no longer a "realistic" option.

This does not mean that a pacifist ethics is based on the moral perfection of Christians. As Cavanaugh puts it, "Church resistance to violence should not be based on a view of the church as a perfect society, but rather on the penitential recognition that we are incapable of using violence justly" (2011, 5). We don't rule out the use of violence because we claim to be more upright, more holy, more just—just the opposite: we confess our inability to use violence righteously.

This also does not mean that the Christian life is passive or inactive, or that it is irrelevant to the real world of politics, economics, shopping, playing, and war. The refusal of violence is not a withdrawal from public life or from politics. A pacifist ethics *is* a political option. By refusing to follow the path of violence, a pacifist ethics of evangelism counters and disarms empire by unmasking the stories that sustain it and ultimately subverts empire by offering a peaceful story and people. Christians do not build or create the reign of God. Rather, we faithfully witness to it in the distinctive way we reorder our loyalties, priorities, and relationships. In the way power and resources are shared and distributed among us, we make visible and habitable a new peoplehood, a Spirit-created social option available to the world here and now.

However accommodated, however domesticated, there have always been Christians who at various times and in various places practiced evangelism in ways that could be considered counterimperial. But then as now, Christians primarily invite others to follow Jesus by following him themselves—his politics, his economics, and his way of responding to the powers by refusing to fight violence with violence.

Though the world is indeed fallen, there is no reason to believe that God has abandoned us. Evangelism is always a hopeful enterprise, and one of the great things about hope is that it trains us to look for outbreaks of peace in the most unexpected places, including the military. But hope is, of course, absurd. In fact, as Thornton Wilder rightly said, "Hope, like faith, is nothing if it is not courageous; it is nothing if it is not ridiculous" (1967, 71). Our task as Christians is to better learn how to clarify and exemplify our ridiculous hope so that it can be recognized as good news. Ultimately that will mean corporately embodying this hope as a distinctive people—living before the world as people of promise and peace. As Paul puts it, "For in hope we were saved. Now hope that is seen is not hope. For who hopes for what is seen? But if we hope for what we do not see, we wait for it with patience" (Rom. 8:24–25).

7

The Pluralism of Consumer Culture

The mechanisms used by nations and empires to seek and achieve influence and control are often political and military in nature; they are also always economic. In our time, economic power, secured by military means, is often the primary way empire extends itself throughout the world. Empire conquers not merely nations but markets. One could argue that our formation by the market is so comprehensive and systematic that it rivals our formation by empire, but that would be to say too little, as market and empire go hand in hand. Empire has always exercised political influence on, if not control of, the economies of those it subjugates or purports to represent. In our time, however, though the political shapes and controls the economic, the economic also shapes and controls the political, so powerful and deterritorialized is the market in imperial affairs throughout the world. It is no accident that when al-Qaeda planned its attack on 9/11, it chose not only the Pentagon and the White House but also

the World Trade Center, three of the most powerful symbols of
modern empire.

Worship and the Marketplace

What we might call "market rationality" is in our society roughly
equivalent to the air we breathe, and virtually every aspect of our
lives is submitted to its logic. The church is no exception, and it
has filled its lungs to capacity with this air. Nowhere is this truer
than when it comes to worship, which in some quarters has become so consumer oriented, so customized around what is useful,
attractive, or entertaining, that it ceases to be an ecclesial practice
by which we are formed into Christ; it becomes instead a practice
by which the church is formed into an extension of the market.
As Paul Wadell says,

> Much of contemporary worship has been taken over by the logic
> and categories of consumerism. In the logic of consumerism, the
> pastor or minister becomes not the leader of a community of faith
> who is summoned to call that community to greater faithfulness
> in discipleship but a salesperson trying to market a product to a
> congregation. The congregation in turn sees itself not primarily as
> the people of God but as a group of diverse and very demanding
> consumers whose needs often conflict. When worship becomes cap-
> tive to consumerism, you need a God people will like and a message
> they are willing to buy. . . . Wherever such congregations exist we
> find not a community of the friends of God but an assortment of
> isolated and often divisive individuals whose lives are connected by
> nothing more than the slender thread of choice. (2002, 21)

Rather than an activity that unleashes the Spirit into our midst,
worship then becomes a means for either keeping God at a comfortable distance or reducing God to our "buddy." In both cases,
it asks nothing substantial of us. A crucial challenge for practicing
worship or evangelism is whether these practices can resist, not

to mention challenge, the powerful and formative processes of the market. Modern nation-states often succeed in subordinating the church to their own ends in order to maintain a monopoly on power and control over the bodies of the individuals whose rights and freedoms they profess to secure. But the market has succeeded in subordinating both the state and the church to its own ends.

Evangelism as a Competitive Practice

I do not intend here to construct an ethical critique of a free-market economics or to argue for the superiority of one economic system over another. My aim is much more modest—to consider how evangelism is habituated as a competitive practice within the context of consumer culture. To consider this, we must realize that the marketplace enacts its own pluralism (remembering that *pluralisms* are really about *unities*) through a logic of exchange and dynamics such as commodification, branding, and consumption. I also aim to explore how Christian witness is made beautiful, alive, and habitable when rooted in an alternative economics and enacted around the table of Christ, a table that is to be extended to all our other tables.

It is virtually impossible to neatly sum up how the values and practices of consumer culture form us as a people. But perhaps it is not so difficult to see how consumer culture habituates evangelism as a competitive practice, formed as it often is by a marketplace rationality. Everything about the marketplace breeds competition. It is possible to think of the market rather narrowly in terms of its effect on prices, the stock market, interest rates, or currencies. It is more difficult to detect the often imperceptible ways the market serves as something more like a comprehensive *habitus*, or form of life. This marketplace logic extends to literally every aspect of our lives—from the way we make ethical judgments in terms of costs versus benefits to the way we value objects and people in terms of their *exchange* value. Thus the services of a professional quarterback have a higher exchange value than those of a schoolteacher.

Pluralism and Our Formation as Consumers

The first thing to note is the remarkable breadth of the market-place's formation, a good example being how the market forms us into competitive selves and thereby pits us against one another. Recent commercials from eBay's "shop victoriously" campaign featured several different thirty-second commercials, each of which spotlighted an item and a group of people racing to win it and become the victor. One ad features a group of people racing like greyhounds toward the finish line to win an old radio. A second features a group of people in a fox hunt for an Evel Knievel lunchbox. Yet another shows a man winning a state-fair game and choosing a "red one"—a red Mustang convertible. eBay's pitch in these commercials? "It's better when you win it." The not-so-subtle message of the ads corresponds exactly to the reality—we simply cannot get enough competition in our lives. Competition has always been built into capitalist modes of production, sales, and marketing. Now it has been extended to our shopping and our purchasing as well. A purchase is more satisfying, says eBay, when you beat out someone else for it. Not only did *you* get it; *they* didn't.

But beyond this basic level in which the marketplace forms us as competitive selves, we should also consider the particular construction of pluralism within the marketplace. Pluralism is a value in and of itself because a preoccupation with choice is at the heart of consumer formation. Religion is far from an exception to the rule; indeed, religious traditions have proven themselves especially susceptible to the processes of commodification as their leaders, beliefs, and institutions are disciplined for the market, and their symbol systems, practices, narratives, and material objects are exploited for marketing purposes. As Peter Berger puts it,

> The religious tradition, which previously could be authoritatively imposed, now has to be marketed. It must be "sold" to a clientele that is no longer constrained to "buy." The pluralist situation is, above all, *a market situation*. In it, the religious institutions become

marketing agencies and the religious traditions become consumer commodities. (1967, 138)

Vincent Miller in *Consuming Religion* points out that commodification has two important and interrelated consequences for religion—and, I might add, for how pluralism is constructed by the marketplace. First, "elements of religious traditions are fragmented into discrete, free-floating signifiers abstracted from their interconnections with other doctrines, symbols, and practices" (2004, 3). This can take place with various artifacts: prayer beads, jewelry and pendants (such as the crucifix), tattoos and other body markings, dress, statues, action figures, and toys (78). Miller argues that removing elements from their traditional context "weakens their ability to impact the concrete practice of daily life." This dislocation strips objects, symbols, and practices from their belief systems, thus "they are more readily put to other uses, as shallow signifiers of whatever religious sentiment we desire" (3).

A second consequence of the commodification of religion, says Miller, has to do with practices and how they are uprooted and cut off from their relationships to the communities and traditions that produced them. Examples include prayers, rituals, liturgies, narratives, music, or perhaps even meditation practices, yoga, or Tantric sexual practices (79). When such practices are disconnected from their original systems of meaning and communities of practice, they become something else. What remains is what is "usable," thus depriving those practices of the connective tissues in religious traditions that give them formative power in daily life.

The popular "coexist" bumper sticker is a microcosm of the kind of pluralism constructed by consumer culture. All religions are made equal by consumerism, but not because they represent multiple paths leading to the same ultimate reality as pluralistic theologians have hypothesized. Rather, equality within consumer culture means that religious symbols, narratives, and practices are equally capable of being constructed as elements of a brand and

consumed as disposable commodities—to use Miller's words, as "things to be played with, explored, tried on, and, in the end, discarded" (6). So, for example, we find the images of the Dalai Lama or Gandhi in Apple computer advertisements with the tagline "Think different." Moses and Jesus action figures now surface in a child's toy chest alongside the Little Mermaid or Mr. Potato Head. Miller emphasizes that the problem relates to "the context and framing of religious discourse, not with the content of that discourse itself." He explains, "I'm confident that Luke can out-narrate A. A. Milne. He is not, however, given the chance, because the context of consumer culture does not construct the relationship between the two as conflict. We are certainly incited to choose, but choices are not exclusive. Choose and choose again. Jesus, Pooh, and the Lion King as well. *Gloria in Excelsis Deo! Hakuna Matata!*" (6).

The Unity of the Marketplace

In consumer culture, religious pluralism is constructed by imposing onto the plurality of religions the unity of the marketplace. Jean Baudrillard illustrates this point by comparing the modern "super shopping center" to the Roman Pantheon, which once assembled the gods of the world in a syncretism all under one massive dome. The shopping center is "our new pantheon, our pandemonium," which "brings together all the gods, or demons, of consumption" (1988, 38).

According to Miller, this marketplace unity is accomplished through two interrelated dynamics whereby, first, "traditions are pillaged for their symbolic content, which is then repackaged and recontextualized in a way that jettisons their communal, ethical, and political consequences" (84). To be sure, the religious pluralism coordinated by consumer culture values and makes space for religious traditions, especially in relation to their symbolic imagery, so it appears to offer us a vast retrieval of traditions—a "divine deli" as John Berthrong has termed it (1999). Alongside this process of valuation and retrieval, however, is a second process: abstraction. What is marketable is abstracted from a tradition, and then its more demanding and exclusive dimensions (such as doctrine, institutions, and the social patterns that inform daily practice) are dismissed.

Miller goes on to depict consumer capitalism as having an "insatiable hunger." This hunger grasps anything marketable or consumable, whether that be persons, cultural elements, or religion, and commodifies them. So what were once meaningful cultural practices, beliefs, or systems are "hollow[ed] out. . . . Exchange demands interchangeability, equivalence. . . . Objects must now function outside of their original contexts" (77). The pluralism described here is precisely what you'll find in the now cliché claim of Westerners to be "spiritual but not religious." That spirituality is fed via an unprecedented exposure to religious diversity through the internet, which can generate, on one hand, a fundamentalist or authoritarian reaction to pluralism that emphasizes absolute truth; on the other hand, it can lead to a more consumerist embrace of choice in which a spirit of eclecticism prevails as people cobble together their own "designer" spirituality from a variety of religious traditions (cf. Leland 2000).

What is important, however, is *how* religious traditions are retrieved, engaged, and employed within the logic of the marketplace, a logic that lifts the practices, symbols, and stories of those traditions out of their original contexts. By eroding the coherence of the traditions and disconnecting them from practices, not only is their capacity for forming people's daily lives undercut, but the traditions themselves are co-opted by the dominant values, assumptions, and practices of the wider culture (cf. Miller, 91).

Some important work is done here that should not be written off as merely shallow or narcissistic, especially insofar as religion begins to show up in new places and new leverage is discovered for calling into question longstanding and oppressive religious monopolies. Possibilities are also opened for the mediation of religion by new kinds of people and for creative experimentation in religious practices (Miller, 76–77). But while consumer pluralism heightens exposure to diverse religious traditions, the capacity for those traditions to pose a serious challenge to the status quo is diminished as is a sustainable commitment to those traditions. Consumer culture may render a religious tradition more accessible, but our relationship to that tradition remains one of "shoppers" and "consumers." We engage that tradition superficially as a disposable commodity and we do so with a diminished capacity to inform and sustain the concrete practice of life.

This hollowing out of religious traditions is perfectly compatible with the imperial devaluing of the particular and of place (see chap. 3). A good example of the devaluing and commodification of place is the popular reality TV series *Survivor*, which is filmed in diverse and exotic locales across the globe. But it uses technologies that actually diminish the distinctiveness of each place so that what the viewer is offered is the "general elsewhere" of "other places" and "other people" (Biressi and Nunn 2005, 13). What unifies this plurality of phenomena are the commodification processes by which they have been made available to us.

Of course, there have always been plenty of ways that religious traditions have been fragmented, rendered incoherent, or disciplined so that their capacity for challenging the status quo is eroded—for example, by imperial power, racism, and sexism. There is no good reason to pretend that religions have in consumer culture met their first or greatest challenge. It is also true that the process of lifting practices, symbols, and beliefs out of their

traditional homes is not just due to the demands of the marketplace; but it is also due, in part, to urbanization and advances in
communication and travel, which produce a freedom from particularity that is also a rootlessness.

But it is worth noticing two things. First, in this system the
dynamics of commodification create a pluralism by reducing the
value of religious traditions to their exchange value—by "hollowing them out" so that they are equivalent and interchangeable.
Second, religious traditions themselves have become habituated
to such pluralism by incorporating the dynamics of commodification and consumption into their own practices. So, for example,
when evangelism is undertaken as a competition for space within
this pluralism, it finds itself shading out particularities that are
too exclusive or strange in favor of a more generalized spirituality or a vague religiosity that will "sell" and that, to use Miller's
language, "smooths rough edges" (77). Houston-based evangelist
Joel Osteen is one of the more exaggerated versions of this principle. Still, as Osteen's church averages a weekly attendance of
over forty thousand people, his approach to evangelism is worth
noticing. According to Osteen,

> The biggest proof of spiritual growth is when we have to keep build-
> ing bigger and bigger churches to hold all the happy people. We have
> a slogan here at Lakewood: "If you're happy enough, people will
> know where you go to church." Jesus often spoke through smiles
> and that is what we are all about. We don't need to confuse anyone
> with doctrine or theology. That is for old people. If our people
> are anything like me, if I were to preach a sermon based on good
> solid theology, they would only walk away with headaches. (2004)

Admittedly, televangelists like Osteen are slow-moving targets
when critiquing the dynamics of fragmentation, abstraction,
celebrity, and spectacle by which religions are commodified and
disciplined for the market. But those dynamics have a far wider
reach than television sets and megachurches, and they manage

to shape even the most mundane and local dimensions of religious life so that they are available to religious and other shoppers for consumption. We live in a culture of conversion, and the self is also understood in commodified terms; it is something to be constructed, reinvented, and marketed. Thus, the practice of evangelism becomes one more offer of conversion alongside other marketplace options.

Evangelism and Cultural Commodification

It is critically important for us to examine the current practice of evangelism in the context of the cultural patterns of commodification and consumption that shape it. Consumption, as Baudrillard says, is "a system of meaning" that nurtures a preoccupation with the acquisition of objects and possessions—so much so that those objects and possessions no longer merely serve us or meet our needs but rather shape and form our lives (29). Objects, says Baudrillard, are no longer created to mark our lives and rhythms; rather, "we live by their rhythm, according to their incessant cycles. Today, it is we who are observing their birth, fulfillment, and death" (29).

This preoccupation and formation directly opposes the values and beliefs of Christianity, if not most other religious faiths, which have historically pointed out the dangers of material attachments. Jesus's good news for the rich young ruler, for example, was that the path to salvation included shedding possessions and adopting a lifestyle of giving to the poor (Matt. 19:16–22). But perhaps the greatest challenge from consumer culture is not how it fosters greed, a desire to possess, and an attachment to material things but how it generates detachment, a ceaseless movement from one product to another, and a restlessness characterized by the persistent quest for something else, something more (Cavanaugh 2008, xi).

The challenge for practicing evangelism within our consumer culture involves more than finding ways to outbid our preoccupation with consumption, acquisition, and the unique forms of "detachment" to which we end up predisposed. As discussed previously, consumer culture is primarily a way we are positioned as consumers to all value and belief systems. It is "a way of relating to beliefs—a set of *habits of interpretation and use*—that renders the 'content' of beliefs and values less important" (Miller, 1). In other words, the content of the beliefs and values is not what matters most, but how they are engaged or used.

Markets will typically claim to be ethically neutral. Because of this, capitalism can absorb its own critique so that marketers do not fear those who reject consumerist values in the name of simplicity, environmental resilience, or to avoid the dangers of commercialization. Instead, marketers embrace such critiques and position their products as "green," "organic," or as contributing to a "simple lifestyle." As Miller puts it, "Consumer culture seems endlessly capable of turning critique into a marketing hook" (2).

The challenge for Christians who desire to evangelize their world, then, is not to find clever new ways to offer the good news from within a crowded set of available lifestyle options. It is rather that of dehabituating evangelism from the pluralism of consumer culture. For in consumer culture, the good news is positioned as a commodity to be consumed, and Christianity is little more than a brand—a skin-deep image of what we want others to think about us, which hollows out the way of Christ in favor of consumer preferences.

An Evangelistic Economics

Throughout history, there have always been Christians who served as signposts to the good news by visibly embodying a social imagination that breaks from the prevailing economic systems around them. Not that they attempt to compete with those systems or to displace them (though that has sometimes been the case), but they do attempt to be faithful to what they take to be the irreducibly material and economic dimensions of the way of Christ, even if that runs counter to prevailing cultural formations. Evangelistically speaking, these economic dimensions are not an afterthought—something to be addressed once an individual gets "saved." Rather, they are intrinsic to the gospel we both have received and seek to pass on to others. This is no less true today as Christians bear witness to the good news through their shared social existence and in the context of consumer culture.

Not Treating People as Consumers

Christians can do (and have done) at least three things to refuse the pluralism of consumer culture and to offer life in Christ to others as a habitable, albeit countercultural, possibility. First, as a church we can insist on not treating each other as consumers, especially those outside the church to whom we bear witness, give welcome, and offer the way of Christ. In other words, we can refuse to adopt a consumerist orientation and a market rationality in thinking about the mission, work, and worship of the church. This presents a challenge because churches grow when they treat people the way people are accustomed to being treated in the marketplace and now expect to be treated—as consumers and customers. Unfortunately, because church growth is now widely understood as the aim of evangelism and as a sure and certain proof that evangelism is effective, evangelistic practice is especially vulnerable to being structured by a consumerist orientation.

On one level, when we treat people as consumers, we end up yielding to the temptation to hollow out the demands of the gospel so that Christian faith fits into the paradigm of consumer pluralism. People as consumers want a tailor-made faith—one that is an eclectic celebration of their own individual preferences and that enthrones personal choice. We become disposed to positioning the church to ourselves based on habits learned from shopping, whereby we expect sellers to come to us rather than us to them. We expect that the product, the schedule for delivery, the payment, and the ability to return the product revolve around our convenience. Meanwhile faith becomes a consumer commodity.

On another level, the problem with treating people as consumers is an even more insidious capitulation to consumption itself as "a complete system of values, with all that the term implies concerning group integration and social control" (Baudrillard, 49). Consumption in this sense is not something that we all simply do by virtue of the fact that we are humans. It is learned behavior. "Consumer society," says Baudrillard, functions as a "society for the apprenticeship of consumption, for the social indoctrination of consumption," transforming even our labor, our working hours, and our friendships and family relationships by the motivation to consume (49). We learn consumption as a "new morality," as a sort of calculus for making the most important and the most ordinary of our daily life decisions. We work so that we can consume. Consumption becomes the logic of our lives.

Christians are not the only persons of faith who struggle with consumerism. Muslims, Jews, and Hindus in North America likewise seek to keep from being consumed by consumerism. Hindus, for example, have their own "mega-temples," such as the Swaminarayan Akshardham temple in New Delhi that includes "an indoor boat ride, a large-format movie screen, a musical fountain, and a hall of [Disney-like] animatronic characters" (Allen 2006). But evangelistically minded Christians, especially if they have come to understand the logic of evangelism as a logic of production and results, are surely among the most susceptible. Churches that adopt a consumer mentality, whether done strategically or by default given the forces of sheer economic gravity, may well come to discover that they have created a monster, as in the case of pastors Kent Carlson and Mike Lueken. Carlson and Lueken were copastors of Oak Hills Church, an evangelical congregation in the suburbs of Sacramento, California. In their book *Renovation of the Church: What Happens When a Seeker Church Discovers Spiritual Formation*, they document their difficult journey of coming to the realization that the "success" of their growing church, built on the Willow Creek "seeker church" model, was predicated on persons relating to the church as consumers and, in turn, their own transformation as evangelistically minded pastors into "providers of religious goods" (2011, 14). As Carlson and Lueken say, "When we structure a church around attracting people to cutting-edge, entertaining, interesting, inspirational and always-growing services and ministries, there is simply no room for letting up" (27). The monster, once created, demands to be fed.

The story of Oak Hills Church is the story of a church learning to follow the Spirit, even if that means a decline in attendance. If these two pastors are correct, the more important question for the church and its leaders today is not how to extend our reach, grow our numbers, or expand our influence and reputation but how to curb our ambitions, or as they put it, how to become "incarnational" rather than "attractional." Carlson and Lueken suggest that reducing such ambition means reducing the pastors' public exposure (having their faces and names everywhere, for example). "We must give ourselves to small and insignificant deeds that nobody knows about. And then must resolve to never humbly work them into a sermon. . . . We can visit at the local convalescent hospital. We can clean a toilet" (86).

In contrast to consumer culture, which is a "society for the apprenticeship of consumption," the church is constituted by the Spirit as the body of Christ and empowered to offer a very different apprenticeship—a different formation that, instead of simply giving people what they want, is a school for the cultivation of new desires (Baudrillard, 49). That formation is, as Carlson and Lueken insist, a "spiritual formation," but it is spiritual because it is a formation that includes the whole of our lives. The fact that the way of Christ includes the material and corporate rather than only the private and interior makes it no less spiritual, for *spiritual* here does not stand in contrast to *material*.

Offering an Alternative, "Saving" Economics

A second way Christians can bear witness to the way of Christ is to provide a soteriological frame for the alternative economics that are intrinsic to that way as "saving." In highlighting this second point, I return to the emphasis in earlier chapters on the ecclesiality of salvation and on the inescapably material, economic, and political dimensions of the way of Christ. To review my earlier suggestions, the economic dimensions of the good news are not merely an implication of a prior and interior salvation that takes place when persons allow Jesus "into their hearts." For Christians, salvation names not so much a private experience but our incorporation into Christ's body and into Christ's way. But the way of Christ is nothing if not material, social, and economic. Evangelism, by extension, is the corporate and embodied offer of Christ's way.

Here I deliberately advocate for an understanding of evangelism that refuses to bifurcate faith and economics, or the personal and the corporate, as some theologies of evangelism do. A good example of the latter is the work of Ronald J. Sider, who has nonetheless done more than most evangelical authors to advocate that Christians ought to give themselves to the work of changing unjust social and economic structures in the world. I have nothing but respect for Sider, and his book *Rich Christians in an Age of Hunger* (2005a) was life-changing in my own theological and vocational development. In his book *One-Sided Christianity?*, Sider argues against prioritizing either evangelism or social action in ways that result in one devaluing the other. At the same time, these two practices need to be understood as distinct. Evangelism is not the same thing as social action, contends Sider, for it arises from different intentions than social action does, just as it leads to different outcomes than social action does (1993, 162–63). Evangelism is closely related to social action in all sorts of ways, but "it is confusing and misleading to call that work evangelism" (161).

Sider does not intend to demote social action in this way; on the contrary, the sharp distinction he wishes to draw between evangelism and social action is "in order to protect the integrity of social action" (163). He has no interest, thankfully, in social action being used as some sort of surreptitious tool for evangelism or construed as "pre-evangelism." But for Sider, Christ's invitation to become disciples, to be saved, is addressed to individuals not social structures, to persons not communities, and "only persons can become disciples of Christ" (162). Sider goes on to argue that social structures could be in great shape and yet you might "still be in active rebellion against God and on your way to eternal separation from God." By contrast, you might be suffering starvation and yet your personal relationship with Christ will guarantee your eternal life (162).

At this point, Sider's evangelical commitments begin to take over, and it becomes clear that his argument rests on the now standard consensus within evangelicalism that salvation is primarily about the individual, is other-worldly in orientation (focused on determining one's afterlife status), and is therefore "spiritual" in the narrow sense of being private and interior. What is missing is a robust sense that salvation is inherently social from the outset precisely because it is an incorporation into the body of Christ— a new form of life as God's people in the world. A persistent problem with the evangelical consensus as it has developed over time (remembering that it is a relatively recent invention within modernity) is that it first buys into a bifurcation of the personal and the social, logically prioritizes the former (even if it does not want to denigrate the latter), and thereby inherits all of the impossible wrangling over what to do with the social once one accepts that dualism.

Theologies of evangelism that start with an individualistic and other-worldly understanding of salvation will always struggle with how to "add on" the work of economic and social justice when what matters ultimately is the question of where one spends eternity and the need to secure that for oneself. If, however, salvation is in the first place a "peoplehood" in the here and now, then to talk about salvation is already to talk about our being formed into a new social existence—the church—from which we learn both what it means to be persons and how to act "socially" in the world as a Christ-shaped social body. This new social existence includes an alternative way of ordering our lives together (and thus a distinctive politics) as well as an alternative way of acquiring, managing, and distributing our resources (and thus a distinctive economics). It also includes a new hope and orientation toward the future in that we now place our lives both individually and as a people in God's hands, and thus we are released from the need to try to make sure history comes out right. As Karl Rahner describes hope, it is "the enduring attitude of 'outwards from self' into the uncontrollability of God" (1981, 231). Hope, therefore, is not another name for security or certainty about the future, nor is it really about guaranteeing our own individual welfare. It is about letting go of the need for securities, certainties, and guarantees as we open ourselves up to God.

Christians are not united with Christ by ourselves nor do we find salvation on our own but always in and through the body of Christ, the church. That is why Martin Luther, who surely knew something about personal justification by faith, could at the same time assert that the church is "the mother that begets and bears every Christian through the Word of God" (1959, 416) and that therefore "[the one] who wants to find Christ must first find the church" (1974, 52:39). John Wesley, the founder of Methodism, could likewise insist that "'holy solitaries' is a phrase no more consistent with the gospel than holy adulterers. The gospel of Christ knows of no religion, but social; no holiness but social holiness" (1958, 14:321).

Modeling the Ethics of Christ

A third and more obvious (though certainly the most difficult) thing that Christians can do in refusing the comprehensive formation of consumer culture while opening up life in Christ to others is to model that life before a watching world as individuals, families, and congregations in local contexts. To the extent that our dwelling houses and meeting houses, possessions, spending habits, and economic priorities reflect the surrounding competitiveness and hollowness of consumer culture, we will have nothing to offer the world. We can't just mimic the world around us and then claim to offer people Christ at the same time. Ethics *is* evangelism.

In the West, it is as difficult as anywhere else in the world (if not more difficult) to model, embody, and thereby bear witness to the economic dimensions of Christ's way—to enact covenantal relationships rather than merely contractual exchanges with one another. And yet in a variety of shapes and sizes, communities of Christian hope persist and are newly coming into being. The relationships, practices, habits, and upside-down models of leadership and accountability in these communities open up a new and alternative social and economic space that is offered to the world as good news.

These communities are nothing new in Christianity. We read about them in the New Testament, where the first Christians held all things in common and "would sell their possessions and goods and distribute the proceeds to all, as any had need" (Acts 2:44–45). There are also good indications that these radical practices of economic sharing continued on into the second century. As Tertullian (ca. 160–220) writes,

> Though we have our treasure-chest, it is not made up of purchase-money, as of a religion that has its price. On the monthly day, if he likes, each puts in a small donation; but only if it be his pleasure, and only if he be able: for there is no compulsion; all is voluntary. These gifts are, as it were, piety's deposit fund. For they are not taken thence and spent on feasts, and drinking-bouts, and eating-houses, but to support and bury poor people, to supply the wants of boys and girls destitute of means and parents, and of old persons confined now to the house. . . . But it is mainly the deeds of a

love so noble that lead many to put a brand upon us. *See*, they say, *how they love one another*. . . . One in mind and soul, we do not hesitate to share our earthly goods with one another. All things are common among us but our wives. (1866–72, 46)

Other examples throughout Christian history abound, even if they often represent communities on the margins. Numerous communities have been formed that were inspired by monastic ideals of poverty, charity, simplicity, and accountability. These stretch from early desert communities in the third and fourth centuries, to wandering mendicants who followed the path laid out by Francis of Assisi in the thirteenth century, to Basilian, Dominican, Carmelite, Cistercian, Benedictine, and other religious orders who have established monasteries and convents for centuries. In addition, sixteenth-century reforming groups such as the Mennonites and Hutterites insisted on radical economic sharing and, in some cases, the rejection of private property as a central part of their understanding of salvation and calling to gospel fidelity. John Wesley formed societies, classes, and bands in eighteenth-century England that made personal and social economic considerations central to the process of sanctification to which all Christians are called, not just those who have taken monastic vows. Another more recent model of being church in which any neat separation between spiritual and economic matters is dissolved are the "base communities" that began to spring up in astounding numbers in the mid-twentieth century in Latin America, Africa, and other parts of the world. These communities practice reading Scripture "from below" (from the "base") in ways that challenge customary readings that arise from the standpoint of power and privilege. Incorporating a spiral of action and reflection oriented toward transformation rather than justification of the status quo, these communities represent a challenge to any understanding of salvation that is so privatized, individualized, and rendered other-worldly that it fails to address the economic challenges of our time.

Even this one-paragraph summary, lacking as it is in detail, should imply just how powerful and expansive is the history of Christian communities who have understood the way of Christ to include necessarily (and not merely to imply as an afterthought) an alternative economics. But it is perhaps all the more remarkable to find examples of that understanding lived out today in the context of consumer culture, given its power as a comprehensive "system of meaning" and a "society for the apprenticeship of consumption" (again quoting Baudrillard). In fact, many of the communities mentioned in the previous paragraph are forebears of these contemporary movements, churches, and groups. As a way of concluding this chapter, I will mention a few more recent examples, not as an exercise in holding them up to scrutiny as exemplars or models of perfection. That would be unfair to them. But it is important to emphasize that the way of Christ as an alternative to the pluralism of consumer culture is more than just a theoretical possibility.

Several churches in Washington, DC, have grown out of the Church of the Saviour, which began with the leadership of Gordon Cosby and Mary Campbell Cosby in the late 1940s. In 1960, this church situated itself in a coffeehouse called The Potter's House. Church of the Saviour began as an experiment in taking up the path of Christian discipleship as both an "inward journey" and an "outward journey" (cf. O'Connor 1975), a movement toward greater devotion and "love of God, self, and others," along with a movement toward offering help, restoration, and healing in the world. The church gave birth to a retreat center and has long sought to practice racial reconciliation in its context. It was also the catalyst for a host of ministries that serve the needs of the city. The church describes itself (since 1974) as a "scattered church" comprised of close to a dozen small and independently incorporated faith communities and ministries. So, for example, one of those offshoots called Bread of Life Church places emphasis on attending to the economic dimensions of life in faithful Christian ways. The church describes itself as encouraging "new economic practices and structures" that are beneficial for all, and they see their community as an "attempt to embody alternatives to the way of culture that accumulates, protects and self-secures."[1]

For other Christians, the attempt to live out an alternative economics has taken the form of a communal rule of life. And while this has long been a hallmark of monastic communities, there is no reason to associate it solely with monasticism, thereby removing it from the reach of most Christians. New attention to the ancient practice of living by a rule has been given attention recently by those who envision a new monasticism whereby ordinary Christians band together in shared communities to support one another in living out personal and corporate disciplines such as study, prayer, meditation, simplicity, mission and service, confession, celebration, presence, creation care, or reconciliation. For some, such as the Northumbria Community in the UK, their rule is a twofold commitment to "be available to God and others" and to embrace a call to "intentional, deliberate vulnerability" (Rogers 2017, 145). This entails taking up the practices and disciplines of hospitality, prayer, mission, care, exposure to Scripture, speaking out, and relationship building. Their rule of life is not for the sake of developing a new in-group in relationship to the rest of the world. Rather, as their rule of life states, "We embrace the challenge to live as church without walls, living openly amongst unbelievers and other believers in a way that the life of God in ours can be seen, challenged or questioned" (Askew 2010, 96). The Northumbria Community claims that its commitment to building friendships outside what would otherwise become "Christian ghettos" arises "not with ulterior evangelistic motives, but because we genuinely care" (96). As I understand it, however, this commitment to live Christ's way openly and publicly is the essence of an ethics of evangelism.

1. See http://inwardoutward.org/the-church-of-the-saviour/churches/, under "Bread of Life Church."

A number of other Christian communities have adopted a rule
of life or otherwise attempt to live out a "new monasticism" that
includes alternative economic commitments in ways that are at
once both "ordinary" and "radical" (cf. Claiborne 2006). Some
examples include The Jeremiah Community in Toronto, The Simple Way in Philadelphia, The Crossing in Boston, or the Rutba
House in Durham, North Carolina. In 2004, the Rutba House
published twelve marks of a new monasticism, one of which is
"sharing economic resources with community members and the
needy among us" (2005, xii).

Some Christians attempt to follow the radical economic teachings of Christ by practicing a common purse, or "common treasury," as with members of Reba Place Fellowship, which began in
1957 in Evanston, Illinois. While Christians at Reba Place recognize
that the economic dimensions of Christ's way require corporate
support, encouragement, and accountability, they are also realistic
about the fact that a common purse does not guarantee an end
to selfishness or materialism, nor do they claim to be superior to
other Christians. And yet the common treasury is an attempt to
put into practice economic principles from the teachings of Jesus
and the early church such as renunciation of private ownership
of possessions, trusting God for all of life's necessities, ordering
economic considerations around the primary aim of seeking first
God's reign and righteousness, and freeing money for the poor
and for mission opportunities "where there is no hope of earthly
return" (Vogt 1983).

One final example, that of Catholic Worker communities, illustrates yet another way that the radical welcome extended to
the world by Christians is bound up with a subversive economics
that begins with a "revolution of the heart" and takes the form
of a commitment to nonviolence, voluntary poverty, prayer, and
hospitality to the homeless, hungry, and those set aside or forgotten by the world (Day 1997, 215). There are presently 228 Catholic
Worker communities in the United States and around the world.

The movement began in 1933 against the backdrop of the Great Depression when Dorothy Day began to publish *The Catholic Worker*, a small newspaper advocating for the rights of workers and devoted to nonviolent social change that was simultaneously spiritual and material. With the leadership and inspiration of both Day and Peter Maurin, a social activist and important influence on Day, the Catholic Worker movement began to found "houses of hospitality" for the poor, to engage in social justice work, and to bring about economic and political change in their communities.

The Catholic Worker communities were founded on commitments that have long been known in Christian tradition as "works of mercy." These include seven *corporal works* taken from Jesus's teachings: "feeding the hungry, giving drink to the thirsty, clothing the naked, offering hospitality to the homeless, caring for the sick, visiting the imprisoned, and burying the dead." They also include seven *spiritual works* drawn from the Christian tradition: "admonishing the sinner, instructing the ignorant, counseling the doubtful, comforting the sorrowful, bearing wrongs patiently, forgiving all injuries, and praying for the living and the dead" (Day, 7). Day once wrote that she considered following Christ in these works of mercy "to be the best revolutionary technique and a means for changing the social order rather than perpetuating it" (9). Whether Day would have considered her efforts "evangelism," I cannot know, but I have to agree with Archbishop Jose H. Gomez, who claims that for Day, everything "was rooted in the encounter with Jesus Christ"; she has left a legacy that affirms the best way to live in, transform, and evangelize the world is "to raise up a new generation of saints" (Catholic News Agency 2015). Perhaps it is not unreasonable to imagine that, just as Christ's disciples reported that "he had been made known to them in the breaking of the bread" on the road to Emmaus (Luke 24:35), so also Christ may make himself known today to new disciples in the bread we share with them as his body.

8

Evangelism and Pluralistic Theologies of Religion

There are important similarities between the three kinds of pluralism (imperialist, nationalist, and consumerist) I have described thus far and pluralistic theologies of religion, which claim that all religions are oriented in some way or another toward the same religious object or end (whether that is called "God," "Nirvana," or "Ultimate Reality"). These pluralistic theologies claim that religious truth is not the monopoly of any one religion but is shared to some degree by them all. John Hick, who could justifiably be considered a good representative of this view, claims that the great world faiths are all ways of salvation that attempt to provide contexts for human transformation from "self-centeredness to Reality-centeredness" (1989, 300).

Postcolonial and other critics have highlighted how pluralistic theologies perpetuate colonialist outlooks in ways that diminish differences in favor of transcendent unities or abstracted commonalities, which end up domesticating and commodifying religious traditions. Colonialist discourse, as Kathryn Tanner emphasizes, is uneasy with difference and with the other *as other*. It therefore constructs its "others" by insisting on sameness, uniformity, and identity in essential values, beliefs, and norms, and it does this by presuming to speak from a neutral vantage point that pretends to comprehend a totality (1993, 2–3). As Tanner puts it, "Commonalities, which should be established in and through a process of dialogue, are constructed ahead of time by pluralists to serve as presuppositions for dialogue; pluralists thereby close themselves to what people of other religions might have to say about their account of these commonalities" (2). By focusing on commonalities, pluralists end up diminishing the extent and importance of the differences among the religions. What is more, the generalizations they form by taking on "a global outlook" end up hiding or disguising their own particular starting point, social locations, and perspective (2).

As I noted earlier in this book, even the use of the word "religion" itself participates in the colonialist dynamic described by Tanner. The word is notoriously difficult to define, and its usage to cover traditions of thought and practice as diverse as Christianity, Buddhism, Confucianism, and civil religion already enacts a metanarrative that is employed for the sake of comparison and evaluation. As John Milbank has said, "It is clear that other religions were taken by Christian thinkers to be species of the genus 'religion,' because these thinkers systematically subsumed alien cultural phenomena under categories which comprise western notions of what constitutes religious thought and practice" (1990, 176). Alister McGrath goes so far as to claim that "it has never been shown that the different world religions share a common subject matter" (2010, 112).

McGrath goes on to remind us that the very assertion that all religions are responses to the same ultimate reality is not so much a claim about the insights of various religions as about the all-knowing pluralist. To make this point, McGrath reminds his readers of Lesslie Newbigin's insight about the "elephant story" employed by pluralists:

In the famous story of the blind men and the elephant . . . the real point of the story is constantly overlooked. The story is told from the point of view of the king and his courtiers, who are not blind but can see that the blind men are unable to grasp the full reality of the elephant and are only able to get hold of part of it. The story is constantly told in order to neutralize the affirmations of the great religions, to suggest that they learn humility and recognize that none of them can have more than one aspect of the truth. But, of course, the real point of the story is exactly the opposite. If the king were also blind, there would be no story. The story is told by the king, and it is the immensely arrogant claim of one who sees the full truth, which all the world's religions are only groping after. It embodies the claim to know the full reality which relativizes all the claims of the religions. (Newbigin 1989, 9–10)

In his formidable response to Hick and Knitter's volume *The Myth of Christian Uniqueness* (2005), Kenneth Surin similarly argues that the writings of pluralists and inclusivists like Hick, William Cantwell Smith, or Karl Rahner pretend to occupy a "global space" that "effectively incorporates and thereby dissolves, the localized and oppositional 'spaces' of people like peasants in Malaysia" (Surin 1990, 195). Pluralistic theologies are thus a new form of colonialism that have supplanted the "gaze of Europe" with a "global gaze." This gaze understands the diverse practices, beliefs, and texts of the various religions of the world "in what can only be described as a placeless and deculturated kind of way" (196). While this "global gaze" has the merit of releasing us from a provincialism or narrow ethnocentrism in thinking about religions and their relationships to one another, at the same time, "it systematically overlooks the real relations of domination and subordination which make it impossible—politically—for Malaysian peasants or Bolivian miners to reverse or repudiate this gaze" (196).

As discussed earlier, consumer culture lifts religious symbols, beliefs, and practices from their original context and positions them alongside one another, disguising their irreducible differences. Military culture affirms religious plurality while positioning it under the larger canopy of civil religion through the discourse of freedoms and rights. Similarly, pluralistic theologies often participate in the same dynamics of fragmentation, abstraction, and exchange whereby genuine difference is diminished in favor of more global but ultimately colonialist paradigms of evaluation. Pluralistic theologies then become "an expression of a Eurocentric market economy in which ideas, including religious ideas, are reduced to commodities" (Schüssler Fiorenza 2001, 279).

Exclusivists and Pluralists

It is remarkable how contemporary Christian attitudes toward evangelism in pluralistic contexts accept these constructions of pluralism despite very different responses to it. At one extreme, Christian "exclusivists" assert the absolute truth of Christianity, interpret other religions as rivals, and target adherents of those religions for conversion. At the other extreme, Christian "pluralists" (at least in their most well-known versions) interpret other religions as oriented toward the same ultimate goal but traveling along different paths. Thus evangelism is not only unnecessary; it is misguided and arrogant.

Both positions accept "religion" as an overarching genus of which individual religions are species; they compare religions through generalizations about what they hold in common, casting those commonalities largely in soteriological terms. The exclusivist understands Christianity to be the only true way to salvation; the pluralist understands the various quests for salvation to be complementary. But both understand the different species of religion to be doing pretty much the same thing. Therefore, they understand evangelism as staking out (and competing for) space within the limited social imagination of an overarching pluralist narrative. The exclusivist narrates pluralism as an assault on the singular and exclusive truth of Christianity and so performs evangelism as a competitive practice focused on confession of absolute propositions that contradict the absolute propositions of other religions. The pluralist affirms the interchangeability and equivalence of the religions, inevitably substituting dialogue for evangelism. Both accept established commonalities as their starting point on the basis of generalities that privilege their own traditions; and both fail to recognize the extent of the diversity among religions, separating the cultural form of a religion from the content or message of the religion from which it is abstracted.

While the postcolonial and other criticisms of pluralism I have described may well be true of *some* Christian pluralists, they are not true of them all. More radical forms of pluralism, which we might well refer to as "deep" religious pluralism, hold that "religions promote different ends—different salvations— perhaps by virtue of being oriented toward different religious objects, perhaps thought of as different ultimates" (Griffin 2005, 24; see also Heim 1995). This second type of pluralism argues that in several important ways it is wrong to treat religions as all essentially doing the same thing given the very different "salvations" at which they are aimed. Religions, on this more radically pluralistic view, are not simply examples of different paths all going up the same mountain. Rather, it would be better to say that each path represents instead an entirely unique mountain. Because of the unique cultural, linguistic, and practical contexts in which they have developed and in which they are embedded, those mountains are in many respects incommensurable with each other. This is not to deny that one may find similarities or commonalities among religions that, on careful study, can be traced and described; but these cannot be established in advance. What we call "religions" are largely incapable of being placed alongside each other as rivals aimed at the same truth and then judged from some "neutral" standpoint as having more or less arrived at that truth.

A Wesleyan Understanding of Grace and Deep Pluralism

Christian evangelism, especially if it includes the attempt to secure conversions from persons of other religious traditions, is often thought to be incompatible with pluralistic theologies of religion of the type first outlined and critiqued in this chapter. After all, why would anyone evangelize a person from another religious tradition if Christianity has no leg up on the truth? The view of evangelism I defend in this book, however, is compatible with this more radical or "deeper" version of religious pluralism. In other words, the problem of some pluralistic theologies of religion in relation to Christian evangelism is that they are not pluralistic enough, and so impose a false theological or philosophical unity onto religious plurality. That unity undercuts the kind of mutual transformation for which those practicing Christian evangelism rightly seek as they share faith and hope with others and as they also seek forgiveness and open themselves to judgment and correction. A "deep" pluralism, by contrast, is able to preserve the importance of evangelistic witness without accepting the terms of competition intrinsic to the kind of religious absolutism that characterizes exclusivist Christian soteriologies and the theologies of evangelism associated with them.

Advocating for a deep pluralism does not prevent the Christian from viewing other religions in terms belonging to a uniquely Christian vision of reality. My own Wesleyan tradition, for example, would want to claim that God is graciously, universally, and immediately present in every human being and in all circumstances, creating, healing, revealing, saving, and liberating. This vision of God's grace is universal in scope and does indeed project a unity onto plurality. But it does not (or at least it *need* not) yield to the competitiveness engendered by other constructions of unity and plurality, which I have described earlier in this book. This vision of God's grace provides a robust inner logic, rationale, and dynamic to evangelism; embraces difference; and accepts plurality without seeking to conquer it through a prior epistemological unity and the evangelistic apologetics that flows from it. In other words, the unity of grace that is projected onto plurality turns out to be a very different kind of unity from what surfaces in the context of empire, civil religion, and consumer culture.

Grace, as it was imagined by John Wesley, is the prior ("prevenient"), immediate, and universally available offer by God of healing, salvation, and liberation in every human context. Grace may be said to be "supernatural," but since, for Wesley, no person is born in an ungraced state, the distinction between natural and supernatural is purely academic. We are all born graced and no one could even so much as exist whatsoever apart from God's grace. Though grace is prevenient and universal, the operation of grace is nonviolent for Wesley. God is immediately present to all and works by "every moment superintending everything that [God] has made; strongly and sweetly influencing all, and yet without destroying the liberty of [God's] rational creatures" (1984, 4:43). God's will, initiative, and power are asserted emphatically here, but not in a way that controls, negates, or overrides human liberty. For Wesley, God is "willing that all [humans] should be saved yet not willing to force them thereto; willing that [humans] should be saved, yet not as trees or stones but as [humans], as reasonable creatures, endued with understanding to discern what is good and liberty either to accept or refuse it" (1964, 450).

As Wesley says, every part of God's wisdom is "suited to this end . . . to save [us] as [humans]; to set life and death before [us]; and then persuade, not force, [us] to choose life!" (1964, 450). The operation of grace in human life is, therefore, resistible, but it is also irreducibly plural. What is "vulgarly called 'natural conscience,'" according to Wesley, is found in every person, and not only in Christians (1984, 4:163). At the same time, it is precisely because conscience is the product of multiple influences, including God's grace, that humans respond to grace with remarkable variability. Michael Lodahl writes,

> For Wesley, . . . the human conscience is a *con-fluence*, a flowing together: there is the influence, the inflowing, of all our experiences, education, and relationships; there is also the inflowing of God's

own Spirit to quicken, to address, to call, to convict. In practice, indeed in reality, these influences are inseparably intertwined. We find this notion particularly clearly in Wesley's sermon "On Conscience," where he points out that the term's etymology is "to know together with" another. He takes this "other" to be God—but *not* "none other than" God! Hence, on the one hand he rejects the phrase "natural conscience" because "properly speaking, it is not natural, but a supernatural gift of God, above all [God's] natural endowments" [1984, 3:482]. On the other hand, conscience "is that faculty whereby we are at once conscious of our own thoughts, words, and actions, and of their merit or demerit. . . . But this varies exceedingly, according to education and a thousand other circumstances [483]." (2005, 201)

The story Wesley offers of God's prevenient, revealing, creating, saving, and sanctifying grace provides a fully comprehensive framework for interpreting human existence and describing reality. But that story, while it is certainly a metanarrative, should lead us to expect—and to embrace—the plurality that we find in diverse religious traditions. Or at least we find in that story no a priori grounds for rejecting other faiths as flawed or mistaken. We may eventually come to the conclusion that a religion is deficient or destructive in some way (as I have in the case of US civil religion); however, the first thing to be said about other faith traditions is not that they are deficient but that they are different. That difference may even be so radical in some cases as to warrant the assessment that they are not all responding to the same religious object or moving toward the same religious end (cf. Heim).

   Instead, Christians have every reason to stand humbly in the presence of other faith traditions, encountering them on their own terms as much as possible and engaging their adherents in an ad hoc manner that presupposes the historicity, particularity, and distinctiveness of each tradition in every meeting of their respective positions (see Yoder 1994, 242–61). Christians offering the good news to others possess no indubitable foundations in human experience or grand metaphysical schemes on the basis of which they can clinch the universal superiority of that news as good, saving, or true. They have only the particular story they have been given, the particular savior to whom that story points, and the particular community that attempts to embody and enact his good news. But neither dialogue nor evangelism requires such sure foundations anyway, despite the fact that within modernity both are frequently imagined as possible only from within some supposedly wider, neutral, and more universal and all-encompassing horizon greater than any one religion and on the basis of which they may all be compared.

It is only after careful study, respectful dialogue, and a close and sympathetic attention to the rich particularity of a religion's stories, practices, and way of life that one can begin to understand a religion in such a way as to make judgments about its commensurability with Christianity or what the good news might mean in the context of that tradition. Taking seriously religious differences in this way does not prevent Christians from finding God at work in the lives of non-Christians. In fact, given the comprehensiveness of the story we have to tell about grace, we should expect this. But that does not mean that all religions are essentially saying and doing the same thing as Christianity, albeit anonymously or implicitly. The (sometimes radical) differences between Christianity and other religious traditions need not be disguised or denied as a prerequisite to either dialogue or evangelism. What is required is both a willingness to bear faithful witness to Christ and a genuine openness to the non-Christian, even to the extent that, as Newbigin suggests, "we are prepared to receive judgment and correction" and thus to put our own Christian faith at risk (1995, 182).

The approach to evangelism I advocate in the context of religious pluralism, then, takes seriously the universality of grace; it also takes seriously the nonviolent nature of grace as a gift along with the unavoidable acceptance of historical relativity, particularity, and difference. At the same time, despite the fact that the operation of grace is irreducibly plural, given what Wesley describes as "a thousand other circumstances," this approach to pluralism does not shrink from commending its truth to others as good news even while it seeks repentantly to receive correction from others. Christian evangelism must ever remain uninterested in competing for space in the world or triumphing over other faiths in a crowded market of options. In one sense, the good news of Jesus Christ can never be at home. Its truth will always be strange and out of place; it is news that risks distortion the moment it is spoken. In another sense, its place in the world is already secure—in derelict mangers and abandoned leper colonies, among the poor and those tormented by demons, at weddings with friends and dinner in the houses of known sinners, at the foot of the cross and the door of the tomb.

9

Evangelism and Beauty

You yourselves are our letter, written on our hearts, to be known and read by all; and you show that you are a letter of Christ, prepared by us, written not with ink but with the Spirit of the living God, not on tablets of stone but on tablets of human hearts.

2 Corinthians 3:2–3

Many people in our world, both Christian and non-Christian, perceive evangelism as an ugly practice—wordy, arrogant, desperate, and competitive, governed by a logic of production, and disconnected from beauty. And yet Isaiah 52:7 records, "How beautiful upon the mountains are the feet of the messenger who announces peace, who brings good news, who announces salvation, who says to Zion, 'Your God reigns.'" The practice of evangelism could very much use a reconnection to beauty. And when it's reconnected to beauty, we may find that evangelism becomes more a work of art, embodiment, and imagination than an exchange of information or a technology designed to secure results. As Russell Reno puts it, "In Christ we are not overpowered by God as a sublime truth; we are romanced by God as pure beauty" (2004, 51).

If David Kinnaman and Gabe Lyons's research is accurate, Christians have an "image problem," a perception, especially among young people ages sixteen to twenty-nine, that Christians are hypocritical, insincere, antihomosexual, sheltered, too political, judgmental, and concerned only with conversions—all of which boils down to a one-word description: Christians are "unChristian" (2007). But in arguing for reconnecting evangelism to beauty, I am not trying to manage Christianity's image problem. The challenge is much deeper than that. Evangelism is the practice of witnessing to beauty—not a beauty we might possess, grasp, buy, sell, master, or contain, or that we are in a position to withhold from some and bestow on others. For we are in no more a position to control or contain beauty than we are able to control or contain a sunset. True beauty always grasps us rather than our grasping it. And though we might recognize it, reflect it, and even participate in it, beauty somehow always exceeds us and defies our attempts to contain it.

Philosophers and theologians have long spoken of the three transcendentals: the good, the true, and the beautiful. And these are said to be interchangeable in some sense. What is good is both beautiful and true; what is beautiful is both true and good; and what is true is both good and beautiful. Christians believe that the way of Christ is simultaneously the greatest truth, the noblest good, and the most perfect beauty. Beauty, however, is commonly recognized as the more forgotten of the three transcendentals in modernity, and this is especially true of those Protestant traditions that have focused on "the word." As Edwin Muir protested against Calvinism in his poem "The Incarnate One," "The Word made flesh here is made word again" (1960, 228). Roman Catholic, Eastern Orthodox, and indeed many Protestant traditions have long insisted on the importance of art, architecture, painting, color, ornament, bodies, matter, and form in the expression of their faith. Yet some Christian traditions, especially within Protestantism, distrust material objects and think of outward form as hollow, if not idolatrous. Their turn to inward piety and a commitment of the heart have a history of resisting all these and individualizing, spiritualizing, and interiorizing Christian faith—with enormous consequences for evangelism.

Aesthetic Evangelism

To take an aesthetic approach to evangelism is not to move away from words altogether, but to move away from their dominance and to highlight instead themes of incarnation, form, embodiment, and sacramentality. "Matter matters" (Hart 2013, 76). For that reason, perhaps salvation is not best thought of in the first place as a collection of messages to be delivered, received, and then judged and decided on. Perhaps the gospel of Christ is better imagined, engaged, and offered as a form of beauty, as something in which we participate, as something more like a poem.

> A poem, for example, is not read for content. Indeed, the literal reading of a poem kills its meaning. Neither does a poem begin with a thesis sentence from which each point in the sentence is discussed in minute detail. Such a beginning would suggest the writer has a point to communicate thereby reducing the poem to a mere message. Neither information nor communication is the aim of a poem. Rather, a poem must be read line by line. Each line, however, though read as a unique entity must also be read in the faith that it manifests a greater whole. (García-Rivera 1999, 7)

What then would it mean to think about evangelism in relation to the more forgotten of the three transcendentals: beauty?

In her provocative book *On Beauty and Being Just*, Elaine Scarry observes, "Beauty brings copies of itself into being" (1999, 3). This simple observation is powerful when contemplated in the context of evangelism, given the fact that evangelism hopes for the begetting, passing along, or reproduction of faith. What do we do when we see a beautiful sunset or a quiet lake reflecting the mountains around it? Quite often we want to take a picture of it, or draw it, or paint it. Wittgenstein says that "when the eye sees something beautiful, the hand wants to draw it" (quoted in Scarry, 3). We stop and stare at beauty, an action that Scarry suggests is the most basic and natural of our responses to beauty (5–6). Something about the beauty of a landscape, a poem, a face, a smell, a song, or a taste inspires its reproduction, and frequently with great passion.

We do not typically reproduce beauty merely for ourselves, moreover. We often do so for others. We buy a postcard of what we have seen and send it to a loved one with the caption "wish you were here." It is as if beauty, once discovered, demands that it be reproduced and shared. Consider again the other transcendentals: When we encounter truth, we are obliged to believe it. When we encounter goodness, we are obliged to enact it. But to what are we obliged when we encounter beauty? Perhaps awe or wonder, but quite often beauty also inspires imitation, reproduction, and begetting. In fact, that for which evangelism properly hopes is precisely that to which beauty inspires us. It is striking then that the practice of evangelism has not more fully engaged the category of beauty in the way we think about and offer the good news—or, as we might better put it, the "beautiful" news. Maybe the very category of "news" already directs us too much toward a construal of the Christian way as something wordy or as primarily a matter of messages and beliefs. But beauty does indeed arrive as something new, or as Scarry puts it, "unprecedented."

A faith born out of a response to beauty inclines organically, naturally, and perhaps even necessarily toward sharing. If Christians do not share their faith or seek to inspire it in others, perhaps the solution is not to berate, cajole, or otherwise "fire up" lukewarm believers so they will go forth knocking on doors, buttonholing passengers sitting next to them on a plane, or passing out tracts at the neighborhood grocery store. Perhaps the Christian faith has become unimaginative and unattractive and somehow disconnected from beauty. When faith is solely preoccupied with truth so that evangelism is aimed at securing *belief* understood as mental assent, perhaps it is no wonder that the average Christian has little interest in going about evangelism when it means convincing people to believe certain things. Many Christians are not sure what they believe; indeed, the number claiming certainty about their beliefs is in decline (see Pew Research Center 2014). Likewise, when faith is preoccupied with goodness, so that evangelism is aimed at securing a particular kind of behavior, it is no surprise that the average Christian has little interest in convincing people to act in certain ways. But when truth and goodness are connected to beauty, faith comes alive.

Scarry says that true beauty has four qualities, each of which, I would suggest, renders beauty an obvious candidate for rethinking evangelism: (1) It is sacred in that it mediates and is transparent to the divine. (2) It is unprecedented in that when we encounter beauty it so often arrives in our perception as new and unparalleled. (3) It is lifesaving in that it seems to reach out to us and "makes life more vivid, animated, living, worth living." And (4) it incites deliberation, filling the mind yet inviting "the search for something beyond itself" (24–25, 29).

Scarry sees the first two as closely intertwined, "for to say that something is 'sacred' is also to say either 'it has no precedent' or 'it has as its only precedent that which is itself unprecedented'" (24). This does not mean that true beauty arrives as something alien or mysterious, though it may indeed be astounding, discomforting, or dissonant. It need not arrive with trumpets and thunder or be accompanied by heavenly choirs. On the contrary, beauty is just as likely experienced as tranquil, organic, or "at home" in our world. It both "belongs" and yet stands out from among the ordinariness around it. The notion that beauty is sacred, then, means that it stands in contrast to the profane—not as the other-worldly stands in contrast to the this-worldly but as a rupture in our everyday experience that signals and mediates an inbreaking of the divine that is at once unsettling and captivating (Otto 1923).

As an encounter with the divine, beauty arrives in our lives as something *new*, as an experience we could not have simply constructed, predicted, calculated, or devised. This insight makes beauty contests a parody if not a profanation of beauty. The unimaginative standards of what passes for beauty in a particular place and time become a mold to press and sculpt various candidates (often quite literally). True beauty provokes us to transformation as it mediates the divine but also as it invites us to search beyond ourselves by placing us in relation to divine dissonances, rhythms, and harmonies (Scarry, 31). Beauty cannot leave us as we were.

This insight about beauty and transformation hints at the deep connection between aesthetics and ethics, two branches of philosophy whose disconnect haunts modernity (united in the very title of Scarry's book, *On Beauty and Being Just*). And insofar as an ethics of evangelism is shaped by beauty, perhaps we can better see how this is an ethics of response and witness. An ethics of evangelism for which beauty is central is not an ethics that identifies ahead of time some end at which we aim (the conversion of our neighbor or church growth, for instance), however noble that aim might be. In this case the ethics of evangelism would be a deliberation on how best to attain that aim "ethically." The ethics of evangelism is instead an ethics of response and witness to a beauty that interrupts and lays claim on us, inviting us outward. It is an ethics of participation in a beauty that sanctifies and transforms.

The Beauty of Christ, the Beauty of Saints

In attempting to connect (or reconnect) evangelism to beauty, it is important that we keep in the foreground the particular and altogether unique understanding of beauty we find in Christ. It is true, of course, that all of nature stands as an evangelistic witness—for as the psalmist says, "The heavens are telling the glory of God; and the firmament proclaims [God's] handiwork"

(Ps. 19:1). And as Paul says in Romans 1:20, "Ever since the creation of the world [God's] eternal power and divine nature, invisible though they are, have been understood and seen through the things [God] has made." At the same time, Christians hold that the beauty of God, a beauty that "saves" us, has a distinctly christological constitution. We do not start with some general, abstract conception of beauty and then hope that by deliberating about it we will eventually arrive at Christian beauty. Likewise, the beauty that evangelism seeks both to embody and to offer does not begin with idealized or sentimentalized forms of beauty. For the Christian, beauty is defined by the life, actions, ministry, welcome, inclusion, suffering, death, and resurrection of Christ. The pattern and form of his life is the pattern and form of beauty.

It is especially critical in our time that Christian beauty be salvaged from its sentimental imitations, which, as Jeremy Begbie convincingly argues, are "emotionally self-indulgent" and avoid "appropriate costly action" (2007, 47). Contemporary Christian piety is awash in sentimentality, whether in art, music, movies, devotional material, sermons, books, or other forms of Christian kitsch ranging from Precious Moments figurines to jewelry and apparel. One problem with Christian sentimentality is that it "misrepresents reality through evading or trivializing evil" (47). Christ-shaped beauty, by contrast, redeems by reaching into the ugliness, horror, and banality of our existence. To be sure, this has often meant that Christians focus on the beauty of Christ on the cross, which can valorize human suffering in ways that permit, if not sanction, the suffering of women, the marginalized, and the poor and that ask them to bear misery, affliction, and abuse as redemptive. The only suffering that may be claimed normative for Christian experience or that may count as a mark of the church is the suffering born of the contradiction that comes with Christian social nonconformity, including nonconformity with all oppressive and patriarchal social orderings that insist on the sacrifices and "redemptive suffering" of the powerless (cf. Luther 1966, 164–67).

Yet another way to think of Christ evangelistically is not so much an exemplification of beauty as an exemplification of a human life that is lived wholly as a witness and response to God's beauty. Christ thus marks out for us a liturgy of participation in beauty, a liturgy that is extended to all in a communion of saints and made possible by the inbreaking of God's love and grace in our lives. Alejandro García-Rivera speaks of liturgy as "the human art which receives Glory and returns Praise" (17). In Christ's life and way, we find the normative and originating liturgy uniting glory and praise, but that liturgy does not occur as a private transaction between Christ and God. Christ is radically available to others and incorporates them into the divine life as part of that liturgy and as a return of praise to God. Christians are called to this very pattern, to bear witness by extending to others an offer of life in Christ. For that reason, "Redemption is not so much a 'rescue mission' for a lost humanity but, rather, the fulfillment of Glory's demand, i.e., the entire creation participating in a liturgy of praise" (19).

The Witness of Saints

Saints enter the picture here as essential agents in the church's evangelistic mission. Saints are those who participate in Christ's liturgy of receiving God's glory and returning praise, and they exemplify what a life looks like when it is given over to God's beauty. This they do in several ways. First, saints point us to Christ through the beauty of their lives. Saints are considered "holy," but that is just another way of saying that they have so given themselves over to God's beauty that they themselves have become transformed. This does not mean that saints are perfect or sinless. Confession and repentance are essential elements of the liturgy of praise. But saints are persons who are fixed on Christ, seek to follow in his footsteps wherever that leads, and are being formed into Christ's body and into a communion of saints. By following in the footsteps of Jesus, the saint provides a material and public witness that is visible and bodily. And that is, after all, the essence of evangelism.

A second feature of the saints' witness has to do with this visibility, which helps us locate the church. In and through the lives of the saints, the church "appears" in a way that violates established boundaries of public and private that would domesticate religion as a private good. Place and time matter when witnessing to beauty. But, as I noted previously, modern empires and the markets entangled with them tend to be deterritorializing, decentered, and oblivious to any fixed boundaries or barriers as they expand their frontiers in an attempt to assimilate and incorporate anything and everything. In the bodies and lives of the saints, these universalizing and totalizing claims are contested. Instead, the saint as a citizen of heaven and by following Christ creates a space where the commonwealth of God can appear. The church is called to be a communion of saints who offer Christ to the world by offering a space and a time in which persons can see and touch the beauty of Christ and be formed into it as members of his body. But to locate that space and time, the church needs—the church *is*—a communion of bodily witnesses who defy the rootlessness and the placelessness of empire and market.

Saints are, in the third place, "an argument" (York 2007, 121). To use the term "argument" in this way is, of course, to reject the hard-and-fast distinction we typically make between the rational and the aesthetic, word and deed, theory and practice. Another way of saying this is that, if Christianity really is true, saints are our best evidence. *Word* and *deed* coincide in the lives of the saints in order to produce *martyria*, "witness." All saints are characterized by *martyria*, therefore, and not just those who end up killed for their witness. Their deaths are not the substance of their witness. It is the saint's life *even unto death* that constitutes a public proclamation and argument.

Fourth, if saints may be said to be "beautiful," that can only be on the basis of a beauty defined by Christ. That is because saints are a living contradiction to the world around them. They may not look all that beautiful to power and privilege. The saint follows Jesus who was, throughout his life, an enemy of the empire. The annunciation and the birth stories of Jesus have clear political and counterimperial dimensions. So too, his crucifixion was the price of imperial nonconformity. And even his resurrection was politically subversive, since it broke the imperial seal placed on the tomb by Pilate and defied the military guard assigned to police it. "Resurrection is against the law" (Wylie-Kellerman 1991, 186). The shape and form of saintly beauty is thus intrinsically nonconformist because Christ's way calls into question and contradicts prevailing social patterns, economic practices, and political structures.

A fifth and final feature of the saint's witness to beauty is its nonviolence, its difference from and resistance to the logic and discourse of empires and nation-states that would have us believe peace is secured through violence. That the ethics of sainthood is an ethics of nonviolence follows, of course, from the fact that the saint follows Christ. And so, in principle at least, this fifth feature of the saint's witness is redundant of the other four. But the nonviolence of the saint is more than simply refusing to meet violence with more violence or to put an end to killing by killing. The saint defies the "othering" discourse of empire and nation-state that undergirds and sustains violence by deeming some persons our "enemies." The way of life of the saint, by showing preference to the lowly, the poor, the stranger, and the outcast, as Jesus did, defies this process of othering and sees in all persons, even the ones persecuting them, a human being loved of God. This love of those whom the empire treats as enemy is something very different from a mere tolerance of difference or a postmodern willingness to "live and let live." It is instead an act of humility that comes from living at the foot of the cross and worshiping a savior who emptied himself.

The saint, therefore, tells a different story from the one underwriting the empire and its violence. It is a story of a God who creates the world in peace and who rules and redeems it through peace. The saint inhabits that story faithfully and in doing so offers it to others as habitable. Saints are, in short, counterimperial evangelists. We are not called to imitate the deaths of those saints who are martyred. We honor them, as John Chrysostom said, by imitating them in the manner of their lives (York, 38). We also honor them by seeking in the first place to become a church capable of recognizing saints in all their different forms. The path of sainthood is not one taken up by a handful of self-preoccupied extremists but is rather the ordinary shape of the faithfulness of those who follow in the way of Jesus and participate in his liturgy of praise and beauty.

The Uselessness of Beauty

Art, broadly understood, is an ally for evangelism given its capacity for moving the whole person and thereby bringing lasting change to the world. But the recovery of an aesthetic approach to evangelism does not mean that Christians should now simply focus on the use of art instead of words or actions as an instrument to secure conversions. Likewise, an aesthetics of evangelism is not really focused on finding ways to "attract" people to the good news. Beauty does, of course, attract. There is an allure to beauty. But evangelism is always both invitational *and subversive*. An evangelism wholly oriented toward the attractional can easily succumb to the consumer orientation I discussed in chapter 7. A thorough rethinking of evangelism is required that attends to the larger gestalt that is the Christian way of life. Beauty resists instrumentalization, resists being turned into a tool or a device that might "succeed" in achieving some end, however legitimate. It is thus important to emphasize the relative uselessness of Christian beauty.

Because of the unprecedented nature of beauty and because beauty cannot be controlled, secured, predicted, or calculated, imagining the practice of evangelism in terms of the offer and experience of beauty is a messy and unpredictable enterprise. The modern preoccupation with technology, science, and economics that unseated beauty in the first place has also shaped the church. Pastors, church leaders, and denominational executives who yearn for "results" are likely to find beauty irrelevant to their preoccupation with metrics, and they may not be able to see, at least in the short term, ways to connect something as ambiguous as beauty to effective evangelistic strategies. Evangelistically, the Christian witness to the beauty of Christ might well take the form of a loving embrace offered in response to the death of a neighbor's child, even when no intelligent answers or neat theological explanations can be offered. No argument or apologetic for the truth of Christianity can compare to a simple act of solidarity and presence that communicates an unfaltering hope. That act *is* evangelism, of course, and it *is* an offer of good news. But it is not always clear that sharing hope beautifully will translate into church growth.

In imagining the task of Christian evangelism, it is always easy to fall back into comfortable patterns, treating Christianity as primarily a belief system and treating evangelism as the chore of getting people to believe things. In this way, we diminish the importance of mystery and imagination in the good news to which we are called to bear witness. Giving people things to believe without offering them the beauty of embodied participation in the body of Christ is like giving a hungry person a recipe instead of a meal. Perhaps this focus on beliefs is why beauty has become so unappealing to the theology and practice of evangelism.

One challenge with an evangelism that emphasizes beauty is that appeals to beauty are so messy, unpredictable, and inevitably less oriented toward measurements of success. Beauty doesn't "work." As Gregory Wolfe suggests, "The indirection of art, with its lack of moralizing and categorizing, strikes the pragmatic mind as being unedifying, and thus as inessential" (2011, 5). Evangelism as an embodied and corporate witness to the beauty of Christ (a witness that is always also a participation) is necessarily material and visible. But the Spirit's activity in the church is an article of faith for which we have no historical guarantees and which we cannot measure quantifiably. All we can do, as Philip said, is to invite people to "come and see" (John 1:46). The question in our time, however, is whether we are giving the world anything to see. This is why Shane Claiborne is exactly right when he says that what we need is not "more churches" but "*a church*" (2006, 103).

The church's evangelistic success, if we can call it that, is always hidden in a threefold way that corresponds to the incarnation, crucifixion, and resurrection of Christ, in which Christian beauty finds its normative pattern, form, and dynamism. In Christ's birth and life, we claim God is Immanuel, "God with us." In the cross of Christ, we claim God has entered into solidarity with those who suffer. And in the resurrection, we claim the promise and anticipation of God's future. In all three, God's presence and activity in the world is material and visible yet hidden in that it can't be predicted, calculated, or secured.

The Plurality of Beauty

One of the guiding questions throughout this book has been about pluralism and the extent to which the pluralisms that present themselves to us in empire, nation-state, and consumer culture—as well as certain theologies of religion—impose unities that wrongly habituate us to think that evangelism must compete for space in the world. When evangelistic practice focuses on getting people to believe certain things (and is thus oriented toward what is "true") or when evangelistic practice begins with moral demands (and is thus oriented toward what is "good"), it tends to be governed by an ethics of uniformity. We want others to believe and act as we do, so evangelism becomes focused on trying to make people like us. In other words, evangelism proceeds from a desire for sameness and replication and a dissatisfaction with otherness and difference.

Christians, of course, are deeply invested in truth, and matters of belief are far from unimportant in evangelistic practice. In our time and especially in the United States, where our current presidential administration speaks casually about "alternative facts," the stakes have been raised for how we understand truth and the extent to which evangelism is oriented toward offering the good news as "truth." These questions will only become more important as we watch truth subordinated to power.

Despite the unfortunate preoccupation of evangelistic practice with uniformity and singularity where truth or morality is concerned, there are certainly exceptions to this and there always have been. The very fact that we have four Gospel accounts of Jesus in the Bible rather than one "harmonized" version testifies to this. John Franke, in his book *Manifold Witness*, attempts to defend the thesis that "the expression of biblical and orthodox Christian faith is inherently and irreducibly pluralist": "The diversity of the Christian faith is not, as some approaches to church and theology might seem to suggest, a problem that needs to be overcome. Instead, this diversity is part of the divine design and intention for the church as the image of God and the body of Christ in the world. Christian plurality is a good thing, not something that needs to be struggled against and overturned" (2009, 7–8).

Franke is not interested in scrapping any distinction between sound doctrine and false teaching, nor does he defend a view that "anything goes" or that Christianity is compatible with any and all beliefs and practices, subject to the whims and preferences of individuals as consumers. His point is that the revelation of God in Jesus Christ cannot be witnessed to without diversity. Says Franke, "This witness is inherently and irreducibly plural. We cannot bear this witness alone: no single individual, no single church, no single culture or tradition. We need each other" (9).

I find Franke's conviction compelling, especially its consequences for evangelism. But I want to go even further in asserting diversity as intrinsic to God's revelation rather than merely characterizing our *witness* to God's revelation. What God has revealed to the world in Israel, Christ, and the church as the body of Christ is a way of living together—a rich tapestry of social patterns, habits, and practices that, while requiring us to remember, critique, reform, and contextualize, nonetheless reveal the beauty of God.

My argument, therefore, is that evangelism is better served by starting with beauty and then moving to the good and the true rather than the other way around. One reason for this is that beauty better makes room for plurality and diversity, opening up for others the possibility of the Christian life as habitable and inspiring, with multiple entry points and paths, and as capable of including mystery, doubt, and moral imperfection. Perhaps a turn to beauty, then, can enliven an ethics of evangelism that makes room for, and indeed nurtures and prizes, difference, contrast, and variation. As already noted, Christian beauty is defined by Christ and his distinctive way. Christ, therefore, provides an aesthetic unity that prevents us from capitulating to the notion that beauty is merely "in the eye of the beholder." And yet for the Christian, the beauty of Christ is intrinsically plural precisely because of the way Christ includes others in his life and body.

The work of García-Rivera is helpful at this point: he traces different ways a theological aesthetics might construe the relation between the "one" and the "many" and thus characterize the aesthetic principle of "unity-in-variety." The Platonic tradition, for example, finds that unity in the category of "forms." The eternal, absolute, and highest forms of Beauty for Plato are nonsensuous and transcend the variety we find in actual things like dogs, tables, or fish. We might liken Plato's forms to blueprints in the realm of ideas that provide the unity of Beauty behind which varied beautiful objects actually appear in different shapes, sizes, colors, and so on.

García-Rivera contrasts this Platonic relationship between beauty and the beautiful with Gerard Manley Hopkins's famous

poem "Pied Beauty," which offers praise and glory to God for all
the diverse phenomena we find in the world:

> Glory be to God for dappled things—
>> For skies of couple-colour as a brinded cow;
>>> For rose-moles all in stipple upon trout that swim;
> Fresh-firecoal chestnut-falls; finches' wings;
>> Landscape plotted and pieced—fold, fallow, and
>> plough;
>> And áll trádes, their gear and tackle and trim.
> All things counter, original, spare, strange;
>> Whatever is fickle, freckled (who knows how?)
>> With swift, slow; sweet, sour; adazzle, dim;
> He fathers-forth whose beauty is past change:
> Praise him. (quoted in García-Rivera, 7)

I will not attempt here to describe or analyze García-Rivera's full
theological aesthetics, which brings together Hispanic-American
theology, American pragmatism and semiotics, and Hans Urs von
Balthasar's theology. But like García-Rivera, I incline toward an
understanding of beauty that moves in a different direction from
what is found in the Platonic tradition, and for which instead
"Beauty's true form . . . reveals itself in *difference* rather than
unity" (28). For García-Rivera, "It is the richness of the unique
and individual that provides the unity for its variety. Plato would
find the 'one' of formal Beauty *in spite of* the appearance of the
'many.' Hopkins finds the 'one' of pied Beauty *because of* the appearance of the 'many'" (28).

Hopkins's poem underscores the rich distinctiveness and particularity of life and of the world in all its beautiful and overflowing
diversity rather than directing our attention to abstract universals
or forms that unite them. On the contrary, the very unity of beauty
is to be found in the richness and fecundity of its own plurality.
An evangelism that takes this plurality seriously is less interested
in asking for uniform assent to a set of doctrines or beliefs and

more interested in attempting to faithfully exemplify the character of God in all its manifold beauty. Evangelism thus requires a "community of the beautiful" whose pattern of life together is a "light to the nations" and a sign to the world of who God is. Evangelistic beauty is premised on the existence of this inclusive community and on the rich plurality of saintly lives. While the beauty of Christ can be announced to the world and while that beauty when announced is saving, the world also needs to be able to touch it, taste it, and try it on. Christ has a body, the church, and that body is constituted by the Holy Spirit as a material witness to the beauty of Christ, however frail and sinful and wide of the mark the church is. To be saved is to be made part of that Christ-shaped beauty by being grafted into the body of Christ. That is why the most evangelistic thing that the church can do in our time is to live beautifully before a watching world.

Epilogue

The Meaninglessness of Apologetics

For I am not ashamed of the gospel; it is the power of God for salvation to everyone who has faith, to the Jew first and also to the Greek. For in it the righteousness of God is revealed through faith for faith; as it is written, "The one who is righteous will live by faith."

Romans 1:16–17

Paul tells the Romans, "I am not ashamed of the gospel." But for Christians who live within the context of a robust and steadily growing religious pluralism, what does it mean to be unashamed of the gospel? Moreover, for those of us who not only live in the midst of religious diversity but who value that diversity and embrace a healthy pluralism in our world, what would it mean to be unashamed of the gospel? If we seek a world where all persons can exercise their faith traditions freely and with respect, shouldn't we exercise some reserve about the gospel, tempering our evangelistic overtures, and restraining or restricting our assertiveness where the good news is concerned?

Technically, a commitment to religious diversity does not mean we would need to be ashamed of the gospel, but there is obvious tension here. Paul's words in Romans 1 have often been taken as a provocation for "in-your-face" evangelism, for refusing to moderate or temper a bold presentation and defense of the gospel in public, especially in the presence of diverse religious beliefs, practices, and opinions. In Boston, for example, lives a man named Bob Whetstone who, since 1993, has walked around outside of Fenway Park, where the Red Sox baseball team plays. He passes out evangelistic tracts and wears large posters draped over his shoulders that proclaim Jesus as Lord and that explain the plan of salvation as he understands it. This plan includes graphic depictions of hell for those who reject God's plan. Whetstone is not ashamed of his conception of the gospel (though I would guess that many Christians are ashamed of him), and I am fairly certain he would find inspiration in Paul's words.

Despite a growing pluralism in many countries, plenty of Christians would like to restore a Christian hegemony or to assert Christianity in the public square. In the US context, this plays out in highly visible ways but also in small ways, such as questions about whether nativity scenes can appear on courthouse lawns or whether a city should refer to the towering lighted tree in its public commons as a "Christmas" tree or a "holiday" tree, so as not to offend non-Christians. Christians who insist that ours is a Christian nation and want to defend a Christian presence and privilege in the public square will quickly tell you that they are "not ashamed of the gospel."

There are those who believe passionately that to evangelize in a pluralistic context is to unabashedly defeat religious rivals to Christianity, if not legislatively or culturally, then by proving Christianity to be true, defending it against objections, and demonstrating its superiority. Especially in a pluralistic context, the temptation to triumph is powerful. We are not ashamed! And this is all the truer in territories of what was once Christendom, where turf is now shared with other faith traditions and perceived, therefore, by some Christians as "contested" territory.

Karl Barth, in his famous commentary *The Epistle to the Romans*, sees the situation quite differently, however. Barth says,

> The Gospel neither requires [people] to engage in the conflict of religions or the conflict of philosophies, nor does it compel them to hold themselves aloof from these controversies. In announcing the limitation of the known world by another that is unknown, the Gospel does not enter into competition with the many attempts to disclose within the known world some more or less unknown and higher form of existence and to make it accessible to [people]. The Gospel is not a truth among other truths. Rather, it sets a question-mark against all truths. The Gospel is not the door but the hinge. . . . Anxiety concerning the victory of the Gospel—that is, Christian Apologetics—is meaningless, because the Gospel is the victory by which the world is overcome. (1933, 35)

For Barth, Christian apologetics is unnecessary for several reasons, and he develops those reasons in dialogue with Paul's words in Romans 1:16–17 (quoted at the beginning of this epilogue). First, the gospel is not a truth among truths. The gospel offers a resounding "no" to the scratching and clawing by which we build our stairways to heaven or fan into flame a residue spark of the divine that is thought to reside within us. The gospel does not need to be defended from within a world of defense nor does it need evangelists who attempt to ensure its triumph from within a world of competition. It is itself a question mark addressed to the whole world of defense and competition. As Barth says, the gospel "does not require representatives with a sense of responsibility, for it is as responsible for those who proclaim it as it is for those to whom it is proclaimed. It is the advocate of both" (1933, 35).

Evangelism—and the apologetics developed in its service—is too often an attempt to close one's fingers around the truth. That Jesus has come to fit so fully within this orientation means that even when Christians proclaim the lordship of Jesus, Jesus has already been made the pinnacle of a competition. The desire to triumph—to convince others, to shore up the truth, to eliminate the refusability of the gospel—is strong. The gospel must be proven useful, and so it is brokered from within a logic of consumption, utility, and exchange. To be a Christian is to be well adjusted, to fit in, to have it all together. But the tighter the grasp, the more truth slips through our fingers like grains of sand.

If Barth is right, however, then the practice of evangelism is less interested in doing whatever it takes to secure conversions, grow churches, or achieve the spread of Christianity around the world. Rather, evangelism is to be practiced as an act of prayer and gratitude in receptive ways and with a posture of vulnerability. While Barth describes this posture as a "no" to the world, Rowan Williams reminds us that standing outside the world of competition as Jesus does, illustrated by his silence before the authorities, actually says "yes" to the world "by refusing the world's own skewed and destructive account of itself" and declining to "settle for the options set before us by the world's managers as the only things possible" (2000, 88).

A second reason Barth claims Christian apologetics is unnecessary or meaningless is that, as Paul says in Romans 1, the gospel is *the power of God* for salvation. Salvation does not lie in our power, and we who would evangelize others need always to remember this. In a sense, as Barth says, "God does not need us." Of course, we are witnesses to God's power—a very unexpected and unusual kind of power it turns out to be. But as Barth reminds us,

> the activity of the community is related to the Gospel only in so far as it is no more than a crater formed by the explosion of a shell and seeks to be no more than a void in which the Gospel reveals itself. The people of Christ, His community know that no sacred word or work or thing exists in its own right: they know only those words and works and things which by their negation are signposts to the Holy One. If anything Christian(!) be unrelated to the

Gospel, it is a human by-product, a dangerous religious survival, a regrettable misunderstanding. For in this case content would be substituted for a void, convex for concave, positive for negative, and the characteristic marks of Christianity would be possession and self-sufficiency rather than deprivation and hope. (1933, 36)

As one who stands in the Wesleyan tradition, I do not entirely share Barth's more negative way of describing God's work in the world and would incline instead toward understanding "the triumphs of God's grace" (as Charles Wesley once described the redeemed) to be more positive in nature. The church is not best described wholly in terms of a void but is rather a material, social, political, and economic reality here and now that heralds, embodies, and becomes the firstfruits of the good news, however inadequate and sinful, however much in need of repentance and forgiveness we may be. Yet Barth is not entirely wrong in affirming that Christian witness is a crater and concave rather than convex. There is also a sense in which "God does not need us," for the gospel does not need our selling, defending, securing, or helping it along. Rather, the very nature of the salvation that God has given the world is corporate and embodied. Salvation is not some individual, interior, or private affair that God enacts on a heavenly plane but is, rather, the formation of a people in the world. That people is constituted by and as a way—a living, breathing, flesh and blood incorporation into Jesus Christ, who is the way. That incorporation *is* the power of God that Paul writes about in Romans 1. To offer the world Jesus is, therefore, to offer the world a people, a church. And in that sense, God does not merely need us; God's creation of an "us" is the whole point.

A third reason Christian apologetics is unnecessary according to Barth is that the gospel is the power of God for salvation to everyone *who has faith* (Rom. 1:16). There is no shortcut to salvation through certainty. Faith need not be blind, but it does not rest on the kind of sure foundations we are tempted to provide it. Nor do the three transcendentals mentioned in the previous chapter supply any such apologetic foundation. The encounter with truth inspires faith, the encounter with goodness inspires love, and the encounter with beauty inspires hope. But the true, the good, and the beautiful are not objective, static perfections that deliver guarantees, especially when viewed through the lens of Christ who, when put on trial before the world's religious, political, and intellectual authorities, was silent.

Those of us who have grown up in Protestant traditions are often taught to think of the doctrine of justification by faith as drawing a sharp contrast between faith and works and from the standpoint of the person coming to faith. But the doctrine of justification by faith also applies to evangelizers. We help people move toward faith not by establishing the certainty of the good news or by attempting to "seal the deal." As Barth puts it, "The Gospel does not expound or recommend itself. It does not negotiate, plead, threaten, or make promises" (1933, 38–39). Paul's "I am not ashamed of the gospel," then, translates into a confidence on the part of evangelizers that the good news does not need us to make everything work out.

The good news is a gift and can only be received by faith. But when the good news is imposed imperially, defended with intellectually airtight arguments, or subjected to the logic of marketplace exchanges, the gift is no longer a gift. The ethics of evangelism, an ethics that is fundamentally self-emptying, gratuitous, and pacifist, becomes instead an ethics of conquering, defending, securing, and grasping. But if the good news really is a gift, if the power unto salvation is God's rather than ours, if beauty rather than winning is the mark of evangelism practiced well, then we can—we must—with joy and confidence stand solely on the promises of Christ, both in brokenness and openness, rejecting all other firm foundations. Where else have we to stand?

References

Allen, Jonathan. 2006. "The Disney Touch at a Hindu Temple." *New York Times*, June 8. http://www.nytimes.com/2006/06/08/travel/08letter.html.

Askew, Pete. 2010. "Pilgrimage: A School of Transformation." In *New Monasticism as Fresh Expression of Church*. Edited by Graham Cray, Ian Mobsby, and Aaron Kennedy, 92–101. Norwich: Canterbury.

Augustine. 1887. *A Treatise Concerning the Correction of the Donatists*. In vol. 4 of *The Nicene and Post-Nicene Fathers*, Series 1. Edited by Philip Schaff. 14 vols. Repr., Peabody, MA: Hendrickson, 1994.

Barth, Karl. 1933. *The Epistle to the Romans*. Translated by Edwyn C. Hoskyns. London: Oxford University Press.

———. 1970. *The Christian Life: Church Dogmatics IV, 4 Lecture Fragments*. London: T&T Clark.

Baudrillard, Jean. 1988. "Consumer Society." In *Jean Baudrillard: Selected Writings*, edited by Mark Poster, 32–59. Stanford, CA: Stanford University Press.

Begbie, Jeremy. 2007. "Beauty, Sentimentality and the Arts." In *The Beauty of God: Theology and the Arts*, edited by Daniel J. Treier, Mark Husband, and Roger Lundin, 45–69. Downers Grove, IL: IVP Academic.

Bell, Daniel. 2001. *Liberation Theology after the End of History: The Refusal to Cease Suffering*. London: Routledge.

Bender, Courtney, and Pamela E. Klassen. 2010. *After Pluralism: Reimagining Religious Engagement*. New York: Columbia University Press.

Bergen, Doris L. 2001. "German Military Chaplains in World War II and the Dilemmas of Legitimacy." *Church History* 70 (2): 232–47.

————. 2004. *The Sword of the Lord: Military Chaplains from the First to the Twenty-First Century*. Notre Dame, IN: University of Notre Dame Press.

Berger, Peter. 1967. *The Sacred Canopy: Elements of a Sociological Theory of Religion*. Garden City, NY: Doubleday.

Berthrong, John. 1999. *The Divine Deli: Religious Identity in the North American Cultural Mosaic*. Maryknoll, NY: Orbis.

Biressi, Anita, and Heather Nunn. 2005. *Reality TV: Realism and Revelation*. London: Wallflower.

Bonhoeffer, Dietrich. 1954. *Life Together*. New York: HarperCollins.

Buchanan, John M. 2003. "Congregation in Uniform: Unselective Service." *Christian Century*, June 14.

Budde, Michael. 2011. *Borders of Baptism: Identities, Allegiances, and the Church*. Eugene, OR: Cascade.

Carlson, Kent, and Mike Lueken. 2011. *Renovation of the Church: What Happens When a Seeker Church Discovers Spiritual Formation*. Downers Grove, IL: IVP.

Carter, Craig A. 2001. *The Politics of the Cross: The Theology and Social Ethics of John Howard Yoder*. Grand Rapids: Brazos.

Catholic News Agency. 2015. "Converted by Love, not Ideology: An Archbishop's Reflection on Dorothy Day." *Catholic News Agency*, May 20. http://www.catholicnewsagency.com/news/converted-by-love-archbishop-gomez-on-what-dorothy-day-can-teach-us-about-holiness-75162/.

Cavanaugh, William T. 1998. *Torture and Eucharist: Theology, Politics, and the Body of Christ*. Oxford: Blackwell.

————. 2008. *Being Consumed: Economics and Christian Desire*. Grand Rapids: Eerdmans.

————. 2011. *Migrations of the Holy: God, State, and the Political Meaning of the Church*. Grand Rapids: Eerdmans.

Claiborne, Shane. 2006. *The Irresistible Revolution: Living as an Ordinary Radical*. Grand Rapids: Zondervan.

Cooperman, Alan. 2005. "Air Force Withdraws Paper for Chaplains." *Washington Post*, October 11.

Cyprian of Carthage. 1931. "To Jubaianus, Concerning the Baptism of Heretics." Epistle 72:21. In vol. 8 of *The Ante-Nicene Fathers*. Edited by Alexander Roberts and James Donaldson. 10 vols. Repr., Peabody, MA: Hendrickson, 1994.

Davison, Andrew, and Alison Milbank. 2010. *For the Parish: A Critique of Fresh Expressions*. London: SCM.

Day, Dorothy. 1997. *Loaves and Fishes*. Maryknoll, NY: Orbis. First published in 1963.

Drazin, Israel, and Cecil B. Currey. 1995. *For God and Country: The History of a Constitutional Challenge to the Army Chaplaincy*. Hoboken, NJ: KTAV Publishing.

Duin, Julia. 2006. "White House to Push Military on Jesus Prayer." *The Washington Times*, January 23.

Franke, John. 2009. *Manifold Witness: The Plurality of Truth*. Nashville: Abingdon.

García-Rivera, Alejandro. 1999. *The Community of the Beautiful: A Theological Aesthetics*. Wilmington, DE: Michael Glazier.

Griffin, David Ray. 2005. "Religious Pluralism: Generic, Identist, and Deep." In *Deep Religious Pluralism*, edited by David Ray Griffin, 3–38. Louisville: Westminster John Knox.

Hansen, Kim Philip. 2012. *Military Chaplains and Religious Diversity*. New York: Palgrave Macmillan.

Hardt, Michael, and Antonio Negri. 2000. *Empire*. Cambridge: Harvard University Press.

Hart, Trevor. 2013. *Between the Image and the Word*. Ashgate Studies in Theology, Imagination and the Arts. Burlington, VT: Ashgate.

Hauerwas, Stanley. 2001. *The Hauerwas Reader*. Durham, NC: Duke University Press.

Hayden, Mark. 2005. *German Military Chaplains in World War II*. Atglen, PA: Schiffer Publishing.

Healy, Nicholas. 2000. *Church, World and the Christian Life: Practical-Prophetic Ecclesiology*. Cambridge: Cambridge University Press.

Heim, S. Mark. 1995. *Salvations: Truth and Difference in Religion*. Maryknoll, NY: Orbis.

Hick, John. 1989. *An Interpretation of Religion*. New Haven: Yale University Press.

Hick, John, and Paul Knitter. 2005. *The Myth of Christian Uniqueness: Toward a Pluralistic Theology of Religions*. Eugene, OR: Wipf and Stock.

Hutchison, William. 2003. *Religious Pluralism in America: The Contentious History of a Founding Ideal*. New Haven: Yale University Press.

Hütter, Reinhard. 2000. *Suffering Divine Things: Theology as Church Practice*. English translation. Grand Rapids: Eerdmans.

Kamarck, Kristy N. 2016. "Diversity, Inclusion, and Equal Opportunity in the Armed Services: Background and Issues for Congress." *Congressional Research Service*, October 13. https://fas.org/sgp/crs/natsec/R44321.pdf.

Keillor, Garrison. 2004. *A Prairie Home Companion*. Radio broadcast, November 6. http://prairiehome.publicradio.org/programs/2004/11/06/.

Kinnaman, David, and Gabe Lyons. 2007. *unChristian: What a New Generation Really Thinks about Christianity . . . and Why It Matters*. Grand Rapids: Baker Books.

Leland, John. 2000. "Searching for a Holy Spirit." *Newsweek*, May 8, 60–63.

Lindbeck, George. 1984. *The Nature of Doctrine: Religion and Theology in a Postliberal Age*. Louisville: Westminster John Knox.

Lodahl, Michael. 2005. "To Whom Belong the Covenants? Whitehead, Wesley, and Wildly Diverse Religious Traditions." In *Deep Religious Pluralism*, edited by David Ray Griffin, 193–209. Louisville: Westminster John Knox.

Luther, Martin. 1959. *The Book of Concord*. Edited and translated by Theodore G. Tappert. Philadelphia: Fortress.

———. 1966. "On the Councils and the Churches." In *Luther's Works*, vol. 41. *Church and Ministry III*, 143–67. Philadelphia: Fortress.

———. 1974. *Luther's Works*. Translated by Charles M. Jacobs. Edited and revised by Eric W. Gritsch. Philadelphia: Fortress.

Marvin, Carolyn, and David W. Ingle. 1996. "Blood Sacrifice and the Nation: Revisiting Civil Religion." In *Journal of the American Academy of Religion* 64 (4): 767–80.

Mason, Anita. 1984. *The Illusionist*. New York: Holt, Rinehart and Winston.

McGrath, Alister. 2010. *Intellectuals Don't Need God and Other Modern Myths: Building Bridges to Faith Through Apologetics*. Grand Rapids: Zondervan.

Milbank, John. 1990. "The End of Dialogue." In *Christian Uniqueness Reconsidered: The Myth of a Pluralistic Theology of Religions*, edited by Galvin D'Costa, 174–91. Faith Meets Faith. Maryknoll, NY: Orbis.

Miller, Vincent J. 2004. *Consuming Religion: Christian Faith and Practice in a Consumer Culture*. New York: Continuum.

Muir, Edwin. 1960. *Collected Poems*. London: Faber and Faber.

Newbigin, Lesslie. 1989. *The Gospel in a Pluralist Society*. Grand Rapids: Eerdmans.

———. 1995. *The Open Secret: An Introduction to the Theology of Mission*. Rev. ed. Grand Rapids: Eerdmans.

O'Connor, Elizabeth. 1975. *Journey Inward, Journey Outward*. New York: HarperCollins.

Osteen, Joel. 2004. "Happy, Happy, Joy, Joy." In *The Door Magazine* (July/ August), interview with Chris Whitehead.

Otto, Rudolf. 1923. *The Idea of the Holy*. New York: Oxford University Press.

Pew Research Center. 2014. *Religious Landscape Study*. Washington, DC: Pew Research Center. www.pewforum.org/religious-landscape-study.

Pulliam, Sarah. 2006. "Military Culture War." *Christianity Today*, April 1. http://www.christianitytoday.com/ct/2006/april/3.23.html.

Rahner, Karl. 1981. *A Rahner Reader*. Edited by Gerald A. McCool. New York: Crossroad.

Reno, Russell R. 2004. "Return to Beauty: Review of *The Beauty of the Infinite*, by David Bentley Hart." In *Touchstone: A Journal of Mere Christianity*, September: 48–51.

Rieger, Joerg. 2007. *Christ and Empire: From Paul to Postcolonial Times*. Minneapolis: Fortress.

Rogers, Melanie. 2017. "Utilizing Availability and Vulnerability to Operationalize Spirituality." In *Practising Spirituality: Reflections on Meaning-making in Personal and Professional Contexts*, edited by Laura Béres, 145–63. London: Palgrave.

Rutba House. 2005. *School(s) for Conversion: 12 Marks of a New Monasticism*. Eugene, OR: Cascade.

Sanneh, Lamin. 2003. *Whose Religion Is Christianity? The Gospel Beyond the West*. Grand Rapids: Eerdmans.

Scarry, Elaine. 1999. *On Beauty and Being Just*. Princeton: Princeton University Press.

Schafer, Susanne M. 2010. "Interfaith School for Military Chaplains Dedicated." *USA Today*, May 7. http://usatoday30.usatoday.com/news/religion/2010-05-07-chaplain-school_N.htm.

Schüssler Fiorenza, Francis. 2001. "Pluralism: A Western Commodity or Justice for the Other?" In *Ethical Monotheism, Past and Present: Essays in Honor of Wendell S. Dietrich*, edited by Theodore M. Vial and Mark A. Hadley, 278–306. Providence: Brown Judaic Studies.

Sherer, Barbara K. 2011. *Chaplaincy at a Crossroads: Fundamentalist Chaplains in a Pluralistic Army*. Strategy Research Project submitted to the US Army War College, Carlisle Barracks, Pennsylvania.

Sider, Ronald J. 1993. *One-Sided Christianity? Uniting the Church to Heal a Lost and Broken World*. Grand Rapids: Zondervan.

————. 2005a. *Rich Christians in an Age of Hunger: Moving from Affluence to Generosity*. New edition. Nashville: Thomas Nelson.

————. 2005b. *The Scandal of the Evangelical Conscience: Why Are Christians Living Just Like the Rest of the World?* Grand Rapids: Baker Books.

Souza Josgrilberg, Rui de. 2006. "Wesley e a experiência crista." *Revista Caminhando* 11 (18):41–54.

Stone, Bryan. 2010. "The Ecclesiality of Mission in the Context of Empire." In *Walk Humbly with the Lord: Church and Mission Engaging Plurality*, edited by Viggo Mortensen and Andreas Østerlund Nielson, 105–12. Grand Rapids: Eerdmans.

————. 2014. "The Missional Church and the Missional Empire." *Didache* 13 (2). http://didache.nazarene.org.

Sugirtharajah, R. S. 2004. "Complacencies and Cul-de-sacs: Christian Theologies and Colonialism." In *Postcolonial Theologies: Divinity and Empire*, edited by Catherine Keller, Michael Nausner, and Mayra Rivera, 22–38. St. Louis: Chalice.

Surin, Kenneth. 1990. "A 'Politics of Speech': Religious Pluralism in the Age of the McDonald's Hamburger." In *Christian Uniqueness Reconsidered: The Myth of a Pluralistic Theology of Religions*, 192–212. Maryknoll, NY: Orbis.

Tanner, Kathryn. 1993. "Respect for Other Religions: A Christian Antidote to Colonialist Discourse." *Modern Theology* 9 (1): 1–18.

Taylor, Charles. 2004. *Modern Social Imaginaries*. Durham, NC: Duke University Press.

Tertullian. 1866–72. "Apology." In vol. 3 of *The Ante-Nicene Fathers: Translations of the Writings of the Fathers down to AD 325*. Edited by Alexander Roberts and James Donaldson, 17–55. Edinburgh: T&T Clark.

Thiessen, Elmer. 2011. *The Ethics of Evangelism: A Philosophical Defense of Proselytizing and Persuasion*. Downers Grove, IL: IVP Academic.

Todd, Andrew. 2013. "Chaplaincy in Contention." In *Military Chaplaincy in Contention: Chaplains, Churches and the Morality of Conflict*, edited by Andrew Todd, 3–17. Farnham, UK: Ashgate.

Totten, Andrew. 2013. "Moral Soldiering and Soldiers' Morale." In *Military Chaplaincy in Contention: Chaplains, Churches and the Morality of Conflict*, edited by Andrew Todd, 19–38. Farnham, UK: Ashgate.

Townsend, Tim. 2011a. "Military Chaplains Are Faith Mismatch for Personnel They Serve." *St. Louis Post-Dispatch*, January 9.

———. 2011b. "Liberty U. Seminary Draws Students, Critics." *St. Louis Post-Dispatch*, January 9.

Vogt, Virgil. 1983. "The Common Treasury." Reba Place Fellowship website, http://www.rebaplacefellowship.org/resources/rpf-literature/the-common-treasury/.

Wadell, Paul J. 2002. *Becoming Friends: Worship, Justice, and the Practice of Christian Friendship*. Grand Rapids: Brazos.

Wells, Samuel, and Ben Quash. 2010. *Introducing Christian Ethics*. Chichester: Wiley-Blackwell.

Wesley, John. 1958. "Preface." *Hymns and Sacred Poems*. In *The Works of John Wesley*, 14:319–22. Jackson edition. Grand Rapids: Zondervan. First published 1739.

———. 1964. "Predestination Calmly Considered." In *John Wesley*, edited by Albert C. Outler, 427–71. New York: Oxford University Press.

———. 1984. *The Works of John Wesley*, begun as "The Oxford Edition of the Works of John Wesley" (Oxford: Clarendon, 1975–83); continued as "The Bicentennial Edition of the Works of John Wesley." Nashville: Abingdon.

Whitt, Jacqueline E. 2012. "Dangerous Liaisons: The Context and Consequences of Operationalizing Military Chaplains." *Military Review* (March–April): 53–63.

Wilder, Thornton. 1967. *The Eighth Day*. New York: Harper & Row.

Williams, Rowan. 2000. *Christ on Trial: How the Gospel Unsettles Our Judgment*. Grand Rapids: Eerdmans.

Winston, Kimberly. 2017. "Defense Department Expands Its List of Recognized Religions." *Religion News Service*, April 21.

Wolfe, Gregory. 2011. *Beauty Will Save the World: Recovering the Human in an Ideological Age*. Wilmington, DE: Intercollegiate Studies Institute.

World Council of Churches (WCC). 1967. "The Church for Others." In *The Church for Others: Two Reports on the Missionary Structure of the Congregation*. Geneva: World Council of Churches.

———. 1997. "Becoming a Christian: The Ecumenical Implications of Our Common Baptism." Faverges, France, January 17–24.

Wylie-Kellerman, Bill. 1991. *Seasons of Faith and Conscience: Kairos, Confession, Liturgy*. Maryknoll, NY: Orbis.

Yoder, John Howard. 1972. *The Politics of Jesus*. Grand Rapids: Eerdmans.

———. 1992. "On Not Being Ashamed of the Gospel: Particularity, Pluralism, and Validation." *Faith and Philosophy* 9 (3): 285–300.

———. 1994. *The Royal Priesthood: Essays Ecclesiastical and Ecumenical*. Scottsdale, PA: Herald.

———. 1997. *For the Nations: Essays Public and Evangelical*. Grand Rapids: Eerdmans.

York, Tripp. 2007. *The Purple Crown: The Politics of Martyrdom*. Scottdale, PA: Herald.

Zeiger, Hans. 2009. "Why Does the U. S. Military Have Chaplains?" *Pepperdine Policy Review* 2. On Pepperdine School of Public Policy website. http://publicpolicy.pepperdine.edu/policy-review/2009v2/why-does-us-military-have-chaplains.htm.

Zizioulas, John. 1985. *Being as Communion*. New York: St. Vladimir's Seminary Press.

Index